THE DIRTY TRUTH ON SOCIAL DRINKING

Published by Lisa Hagan Books 2024

www.lisahaganbooks.com

Copyright © Hadley Sorensen 2024

ISBN: 978-1-945962-62-2

All Rights Reserved. No part of this publication may be reproduced, stored in a retrieval system, or transmitted in any form, or by any means, electronic, mechanical, photocopying, recording or otherwise without the prior permission in writing of the copyright holders, nor be otherwise circulated in any form or binding or cover other than in which it is published and without a similar condition being imposed on the subsequent publisher.

Cover photograph by Lance Asper, Lance@asperpro.com

Cover and interior layout by Simon Hartshorne

THE DIRTY TRUTH ON SOCIAL DRINKING

"EVERYTHING IN MODERATION"
AND OTHER BS

HADLEY SORENSEN

Contents

	Introduction	11
1	The '80s Party Hangover	17
2	A Charmed Life	23
3	Generation Booze	26
4	Finding My Voice	30
5	The Year That Tried to Break Me	36
6	The Rosé That Changed It All	40
7	Give Me All the Lexapro	44
8	The Lady in the Red Car	49
9	"I QUIT"	53
10	Thinking About Change with an Open Mind	60
11	Imposter Syndrome	63
12	What the Hell is Moderation?	67
13	Sharing is Scary	74
14	The Rise and Fall of Badley	79
15	The Shame Swamp	83
16	Learning from Regret	88
17	Kicking Mommy Wine Culture to the Curb	93
18	The Joys of Sober Parenting	101
19	Booze & Marriage	107
20	Letting Go of Fitting In	112
21	Sober is Boring, Right?	116
22	Unlocking FUN After Booze	119

23	Deprive or Thrive	127
24	Exercise Gives Us Superpowers	130
25	Boozy Role Models	136
26	Sober in Paradise	141
27	Daydreaming About My Sobriety	147
28	A New Normal	150
29	Signs it Might Be Time	154
30	Mental Health Red Flags	160
31	Visualizing a Life with Less Alcohol	164
32	Aging Loudly and Gracefully and Forgivingly	168
33	The Lessons I've Learned	171
	Epilogue	174

Book Endorsements

"If you are questioning your relationship with alcohol or are sober curious, Hadley's story is for you. Her authentic, relatable, and vulnerable story allows the reader to feel seen and gives the permission slip to explore their relationship with alcohol. Hadley offers practical advice on the complexities of gray area drinking and its effects on our mental and physical well-being. She also challenges societal norms and encourages readers to make positive changes in their lives. A great addition to your Quit Lit collection!"

—**Meg Geisewite**, bestselling author of *Intoxicating Lies: One Woman's Journey to Freedom from Gray Area Drinking.*

"This book is for anyone who has ever questioned their relationship with alcohol. Hadley feels like your secret best friend, holding your hand through a very vulnerable time in any woman's life."

—**Kelly O'Shea**, President & CEO KOPR

"Hadley's story is as relatable as it is inspiring. Once a fitness influencer known for her love of wine, she found herself needing that nightly drink a little too much. In this heartfelt book, she shares how she swapped her wine glass for a life of sobriety, opening up about the challenges and victories along the way. Hadley's journey is a powerful reminder that behind every 'perfect' social media life can lie unseen struggles. Her candid account offers hope and solidarity to women facing similar battles, encouraging them to find beauty and strength in sobriety."

—**Hilary Phelps**, Creator of The Right Room

"Hadley is a flashlight in the dark, an inspiration to tens of thousands, a voice of reason in all of the madness of our alco-centric culture. I love her work and the message she puts out. She is smart, funny, insightful, and bracingly refreshing."

—**Catherine Gray**, bestselling author of
The Unexpected Joy of Being Sober

"A must-read for any woman who has ever questioned the role alcohol plays in her life and wondered what life would be like without it. Hadley's writing is from the heart, and her honest and vulnerable account of her own alcohol use is one that will resonate with thousands of women across the globe. We don't have to have a 'rock bottom' to decide to quit drinking, and Hadley's inspirational journey laid out in this book gives every woman permission to make a change and create a wonderful life, alcohol-free."

—**Sarah Rusbatch**, author of *Beyond Booze*

Dedication

To my husband, Eric, who has supported me tirelessly and with his whole heart as I embarked on this journey. Thank you for being my rock, my sounding board, and my sanity.

To my amazing, smart, funny, and compassionate boys, who make me want to become the very best version of myself. Thank you for your unwavering belief and love.

And to my parents, who have been my biggest cheerleaders since day one.

Introduction

On Halloween of 2020, deep in the throes of the pandemic, our neighbors gathered outside for a Halloween party since the kids couldn't trick-or-treat. COVID and my husband, Eric's, recent cancer treatments kept my family very isolated. I was thrilled for the chance to see our neighbors and let the kids get dressed up.

Eric was in bed, still reeling from the effects of his miserable daily radiation, so I took the boys outside to play while I had a glass of wine with the adults. We were standing around the fire pit, talking, laughing, and thrilled to be out of our houses and with other humans. The kids were running around in their costumes and having a blast.

We had been outside for an hour when my boys ran in for a drink. A moment later, Eric called my phone, telling me I needed to come in right away. I raced inside, and when I got to him, he told me the boys had come in, visibly upset, telling him that Mommy was drunk. I was flabbergasted. I hadn't even had two glasses of wine—we were all just laughing and enjoying ourselves. There was nothing wild and crazy going on, and—trust me—this is a group that knows how to get wild and crazy.

I talked to each of them, trying to figure out what was going on, as I simultaneously tried to demonstrate that I was, in fact, dead sober. Of course, the more sober you *try* to act, the more ridiculous you look, even if you haven't had a sip. I went to bed that night feeling gutted. Was I a horrible mother? What had I done that made them think I was drunk? Where had they even learned that word?

The next day I learned that one of their buddies taught them what it meant to be "drunk" and declared that all the adults were "getting wasted." This was news to them, so they looked at the grownups through a new lens that night. They didn't quite understand it, but they were on the lookout for us to act weird. They saw me laughing with everyone and thought, "*Oh no, it's happening.*"

This incident might not have been a big deal in isolation, but looking back, the timing seems like fate. Right before the pandemic, I began to question my relationship with alcohol and was feeling as though something was off in the balance of my life. I worried about the example I was setting for my kids as they got old enough to understand drinking and its repercussions. I knew I didn't want them following in my boozy footsteps. Little did I know, I was at a major crossroads, and the next few years would be life-changing in so many ways.

I wasn't a rock-bottom, stumbling-through-life, smelling-like-vodka kind of drinker. No one even suspected that I struggled with it. From the outside, I looked like the perfect suburban mom, and my drinking habits followed normal social conventions. I drank socially, the way we seem to be expected to in today's booze-obsessed culture. Sure, I overdid it sometimes and blacked out occasionally, but everyone thought it was hilarious. It's not like I was alone—lots of people in our circle drank considerably more than I did. If this was all so "normal" though, why did I struggle with it so much? Why did I feel so much shame and regret tied to what was supposed to be a fun, all-American pastime? Why was it eating away at my confidence and my mental health?

I have since learned it's completely normal to struggle with drinking, even if you don't have a severe problem. It turns out that alcohol is a highly addictive, carcinogenic poison. Who knew? It seems crazy to think we *wouldn't* struggle with consuming as much as we're expected to consume.

We tend to assume that anyone with a drinking "problem" fits a specific mold. We imagine someone disheveled, stumbling along with a bottle in a brown paper bag. But problem drinking doesn't have a particular look. It can look like an old friend who appears to have the perfect life and family on Facebook, or a co-worker who always dresses nicely and never misses a deadline. Problems aren't black and white.

Addressing my problematic relationship with alcohol has become one of the great trials of my life. Since I had my first sip at fourteen, something about my relationship with booze felt corrupt. I never felt like I could drink nonchalantly, like so many people seemed to. It was all or nothing for me, and I hated that. Something bad didn't happen every time I drank; it wasn't all darkness and misery. You can bet, though, every time something bad did happen, I had been drinking.

I wasn't physically dependent, and I wasn't even close to rock bottom, but alcohol had a stranglehold on me. I looked around at everyone in my life who was drinking just like me, and they didn't seem to struggle. They didn't appear to be dying on the inside after a normal, drunken Friday night. If they were, they certainly weren't talking about it, so I continued to assume I was the only one wrestling these demons. No one in my circle of friends was raising their hand to say, "Hey, I know drinking this much is supposed to be normal, but it really doesn't feel good to me, and I think something is wrong!"

They all looked as perfect on the outside as I did. I felt like I was the only person experiencing these tumultuous feelings tied to booze, which made me feel like something was wrong with me. It was isolating and scary, so I kept it all stuffed deep inside.

We have learned to keep it quiet, to keep our heads down, and to keep drinking along with the crowd because that's what is expected. We suffer silently because we don't know what else to do. We certainly don't want to admit we might have a problem.

Although I felt alone in my struggles for so long, I now realize that, statistically, that's not possible. Just like people looked at me from the outside and assumed I was picture-perfect, many of the people I was looking at were likely fighting similar battles. We think we know what someone with a problem looks like, and if a person doesn't meet those criteria, we assume they're fine. It's an illusion.

As a society, we drink a *lot*, and if it doesn't feel right to you, or if something about your relationship with alcohol feels icky and wrong, *you are not alone*. If you feel the way I did, I'm here to assure you there is nothing wrong with you. You are not broken. It's more normal than you think. We shouldn't feel ashamed that we can't drink absurd amounts of alcohol with no consequences. Our bodies aren't equipped for that.

My journey over the next few years ultimately led me to eliminate alcohol completely, and it was one of the best decisions of my life. Now, I want to help others understand that anyone is free to decide that alcohol is no longer serving them and walk away. *Anyone* can quit at any time for any reason, and there shouldn't be any shame or stigma associated with it. You don't have to be on the cusp of losing your house or kids, getting DUIs, or watching your life crumble to decide to quit. If your drinking is causing problems in your life, that's all the reason you need. Sobriety is a legitimate option that can be fulfilling beyond belief.

Even if you have just an inkling that alcohol is doing more harm than good in your life, you owe it to yourself to at least explore your options and consider whether you might want to make a change. You do not have to be labeled an *alcoholic* to decide your relationship with alcohol is problematic. We need to care less about the labels and more about the result—a happier, more fulfilling life.

I hope that by sharing my experience, I can show people that Alcohol Use Disorder isn't binary, meaning—either you have a problem, or you don't. It's tricky, nuanced, and sneaky. Alcohol leads us on and pretends it's helping us until we finally realize it has been dragging us down all along. We don't have to wait until our problems are extreme to walk away. We can decide that our lives would be better without it and change the narrative. We don't *need* to hit rock bottom before we change. We can skip all the messy stuff in the middle and step into the best version of ourselves at any time.

I also want to help spread the radical message that binge drinking shouldn't be considered normal anymore. *No* definition of moderation includes getting sloppy, fall-down drunk on Saturday nights. I hope to be part of the movement to glamorize *not* drinking—like we finally did with smoking. Let's at least make it so that we don't need to justify ourselves for choosing to be alcohol-free.

My goal here is to talk about what no one else is talking about. My story is for the millions of moms who suffer through too many hangovers and worry about the priority they grant wine in their lives. I hope to offer a guide for untangling the threads of alcohol that have been woven through the fabric of our lives and remind people that their problems don't need to be extreme to benefit from cutting ties with booze.

So, buckle up and get ready to ride along as I look back over nearly three decades of my life I spent as an enthusiastic drinker.

I'll unpack my toxic relationship with alcohol and the impact it had on me. I'll explain why my decision to lead an alcohol-free life at the age of forty-one was the most powerful move I ever made for myself.

Alcohol was a problem for *me*, so I quit. It's a problem for lots of others, too—maybe even you.

I hope to play even a tiny role in redefining how people think of and define "normal drinking" in our culture, and I pray my words help even one person out there who may struggle with the same issues.

1

The '80s Party Hangover

I woke up face down in bed wearing a tutu, leg warmers, and neon blue eyeshadow. Fake eyelashes were stuck to my cheeks, and it felt like my head was being squeezed in a vise. When I peeled myself off the bed with a groan, my first thought was, *"What in the hell happened?"*

The night before, I'd thrown Eric an epic '80s-themed surprise birthday party. I'd been planning for months and was damn proud of myself for pulling it off. I sent him out of town to our lake house for two days before the party so I could prepare. When he arrived home, I greeted him in full '80s gear, with crimped hair and all. He was stunned when I told him that a catering truck and fifty of our closest friends were on the way. The house looked like the set of an MTV video, and I turned our sunroom into a photo booth full of '80s props. It was perfectly Instagramable.

I set the back porch up as a bar, complete with twinkle lights and electric blue party punch. A friend helped me raid Costco and Total Wine for the booze, and we certainly didn't skimp on the beverage options. Our favorite restaurant transformed our dining room table into a charcuterie board big enough to feed an army.

Everything was perfect. Even though there was an over-the-top '80s theme, this party was going to be *classy*. I promised myself I wouldn't let this be one of those nights I had too much to drink and crossed that invisible line into oblivion. I could have a few cocktails, but I would stay sharp. I would drink "responsibly." I wanted to be the perfect hostess, make sure Eric had a blast, and, most importantly, remember every detail of the party I worked so hard to plan. I even told a few close friends about my goal to stay mostly sober and tasked one of them with reminding me if she noticed me sliding in the opposite direction.

No pressure, right?

The party kicked off perfectly. Everyone raved over the food, the drinks, and the photo booth. The costumes were fantastic. People were dancing, singing to the '80s music, and taking pictures with all the funny props. It was a blast to see our different pockets of family and friends all coming together and having fun. It became apparent quickly that this crowd was going to drink a lot. This was no surprise because our people are F-U-N.

I started true to my word, sipping my wine and soaking in the magic. I was very adult-like, checking in with the caterers and making sure the trash was emptied. I watched my sons having the time of their lives in their costumes, hanging with the grown-ups until their bedtime.

As the night went on, things escalated quickly. A bucket of fireball shooters materialized, and it was all downhill from there. In the blink of an eye, I went from having fun responsibly to completely blacked out.

It was always that way for me. There was a fine line between tipsy but coherent and total darkness. I pretended I knew how to stay on the right side of that line, but it was a moving target. I was self-aware enough to know I didn't want a blackout to be part of the story for this party. I wanted it to be special, and I wanted to remember it—famous last words.

When I scraped myself out of bed the next morning, my brain was foggy but working in overdrive. I panicked as I scrambled to find my fancy Cochlear hearing device, which is not the kind of thing you can replace. Thankfully, it had somehow made its way to the usual spot in my drawer. Then, the heavy fog of shame rolled over me, making it almost impossible to breathe. That dark feeling after a blackout is a unique combination of fear, anxiety, and embarrassment. Did I do anything stupid? Is Eric mad at me? Was everyone else as drunk as I was? Why don't I remember anything? As I tried to piece together anything I could remember from the night's second half, I wondered how on earth I had let this happen. Again.

I slowly limped my way downstairs, trying to assess the damage to my house and body as I went. My brain felt too big for my skull, and my mouth felt like it was full of socks. I stumbled into the family room to find Eric on the couch, looking just as miserable as I felt. I was (selfishly) relieved to find I was not the only one in rough shape. The house looked (and smelled) like a college bar. The kitchen was sticky with spilled drinks. Sequins from someone's costume were practically glued to my hardwood floor, and little red fireball shooter lids were scattered like land mines. It was like a birthday party war zone, and we looked at each other and groaned.

I tentatively started a conversation, trying to feel out whether I'd done anything humiliating or unforgivable. I didn't get the sense anything terrible had happened, but who the hell knew? We compared stories, and I admitted I remembered nothing after a certain point.

Eric had enjoyed himself, which was a huge relief, but he didn't remember everything either. Clearly, this party had been one for the history books. I couldn't stomach cleaning the house in my current condition, so I parked myself on the couch, with the stench of booze seeping from my pores. The kids woke up and joined us downstairs. We told them it would be a lazy day full of movies and video games. A screen time free-for-all while we sat in our own filth, nursing hangovers we were glad the boys didn't understand.

As the day went on, we started getting texts from friends about how much fun they'd had. I tried to hide the cloud of anxiety I was huddled under as we heard from people. I was convinced someone was going to jump out and share a list of awful things I'd said or done.

Much to my relief, I was not, in fact, an outlier. The stories from the night were quickly becoming legends. As friends shared videos and pictures, we discovered why the house was in such terrible shape. People had been dancing on the coffee table, spilling drinks, and taking shots left and right. Eric loved seeing the videos and casting them to the TV for us to watch. I cringed and almost threw up. I would rather die than see a video of myself drunk.

I felt worse and worse as the day went on. It was clear this was a special kind of hangover. As I crawled up to bed for the night, I said those fateful words many of us have uttered during an award-winning hangover: "I'm never drinking again."

On Monday, once I rallied to get the kids off to school, I knew I had to tackle the house. It was the worst cleaning experience of my life. I emptied coolers and scrubbed sticky floors, still feeling foggy, sick, and full of violent regret. I kept finding little pockets of destruction, like fallen pictures in the bathroom and an entire hamburger slider under the sofa. It took all day, and even once I was done, I knew I'd need someone to come in and steam clean the carpets. I looked around and thought, "*HOLY SHIT, aren't we supposed to be adults?*"

I spiraled into a nasty depressive episode that lasted over a week and obviously correlated to my alcohol consumption. That's when I noticed, for the first time, the clear link between drinking and my mental state. How could something that was supposed to be *fun* wreak so much havoc on my physical and mental health? The experience left me with an almost itchy sensation that something needed to change.

While this party and the resulting hangover felt monumental to me, it didn't *seem* to be a big deal to anyone else. It was just a normal weekend experience in our booze-centric, suburban culture. Party, drink too much, hangover, repeat. It seemed to be just a blip on the radar for everyone else who had been there, including my husband. So why the hell did I feel so awful? Why could everyone else seem to drink some water, take some Advil, and move on from their hangover, while I felt like it was the end of the world? I wasn't even the drunkest person at the party.

It seemed like I was experiencing alcohol differently than everyone else. Why did it make me feel so horrible—physically and mentally? Why did it fill me with so much shame and regret? Why did I want to retreat into myself and hide for days afterward when everyone else seemed to laugh it off? Or maybe, just *maybe*, I wasn't the only one who felt this way. Maybe I wasn't the only one wondering why I kept doing this to myself. Maybe it's just that no one was talking about it, and we were all assuming we were the only ones. Maybe the people I thought had their shit together were really coming unhinged on the inside like I was.

After recovering from my hangover, I didn't touch alcohol for the entire month of December. I drank a glass of wine on New Year's Eve, but that was it for most of January. I had a few drinks between January and March 2020, which felt significant. I'd finally found the holy grail: moderation! I felt very smug about this revelation—New Year, New Me!

We didn't know Eric's birthday party would be the last time we would get to see most of our friends in person before the world flipped upside down. The pandemic hit. Schools and life shut down. Things were looking grim as we watched the news each day, trying to understand these new phrases like "fourteen days to flatten the curve" and "social distancing." I still wasn't drinking much because I had *evolved*. I was now an average, responsible, adult drinker.

By mid-April, we realized that fourteen days had come and gone. The curve wasn't flattening, schools weren't re-opening, and things seemed to worsen. Vacations, the kids' sports, and my running races were all canceled. Our family was stuck in the house together non-stop. We were working, eating, sleeping, navigating distance learning, and trying to stay sane while we did it.

Somewhere along the way, without fully realizing it, I screamed, "SCREW IT!" to the progress I'd made and poured a large glass of wine promptly at five o'clock each night while I watched the news. It became my coping mechanism and something to look forward to after surviving another monotonous day of quarantine life.

I felt an incredible level of anxiety. I was anxious about my kids' education, the virus, the future, and the November election, which I expected would make everything worse. Throw in a cancer diagnosis for my husband and a layoff the week before he was supposed to start chemo. It felt like the sky was falling, and I was constantly on the verge of tears.

2

A Charmed Life

I grew up in the Washington, DC, suburbs in the '80s and '90s, and aside from my four years away at Virginia Tech, I've been here ever since. After college, I promptly went to work in the mortgage industry, although it had nothing to do with the psychology degree I had worked so hard for. I was too impatient to earn the graduate degree required for me to become a therapist. I was always eager to get to the next step, hit that next milestone, and to be older and more mature than I was. That trait was both a blessing and a curse.

That first career choice turned out to be a good one because not only was I good at what I did, but it also led me to my husband. As a twenty-three-year-old right out of college, I gave my friend from the office a definitive "hell no!" when she subtly fished, asking if I would ever consider dating a guy with a kid. The rest is history. It turns out I *was* willing to date a guy with a kid, and that kid became one of the best things ever to happen to me.

Eric and I were married in 2005 and moved further out in the DC suburbs. Once again, I was eager for that next stage of life, but I felt strongly I would want to maintain my career after we expanded our family. I was addicted to the corporate ladder. I was driven and ambitious, and I had an intense work ethic—it's that only-child, overachiever mentality. I was determined to be the epitome of a strong working mother.

That changed in a heartbeat when my son, Caden, was born in 2009. I was fortunate to be able to take four months of maternity leave, but the thought of going back to work was painful. Everything I thought I knew about myself went right out the window. I wanted to be home with my baby, and that desire was so intense it shook me to my core. I forced myself to return to the office, convinced I was still too hormonal to make any major life decisions.

Getting back into the swing of things was intense and overwhelming while we both juggled demanding jobs. We dealt with daycare drop-off and pickup for Caden while shuttling my stepson back and forth to school and his mom each day. We were constantly trying to figure out the schedule and fighting over whose meetings were more important.

When I got pregnant with Bryce twelve months later, I knew it couldn't continue. There was no way to keep my head above water with two babies under two. It wasn't worth the financial expense or the mental toll to have them both in daycare while I tried to advance my career. I resigned from my job to stay at home, and I was grateful that we had the means to make that choice. It was the right call for our family, even if it had its ups and downs.

Now we have a house full of sons who bring us so much joy and *so* much potty humor. A fourteen-year-old, twelve-year-old, and a twenty-five-year-old who's already blazing his own trail. Staying home with them was an incredible blessing, and it allowed me the flexibility to chase some new dreams and build a different career.

A few years ago, we reached one of our long-term family goals and purchased a lake house about two hours away from home. It has become our family escape and our ultimate happy place.

By all accounts, I've lived a charmed life, and from the outside, it looked picture-perfect. People assumed I had my act together and often asked how I managed to "do it all." I was the perfect mom of little blonde boys with nice manners. My hair was always perfectly curled. I was a marathon runner, full of inspirational quotes for social media. I baked beautiful cupcakes for school events, and my house was always tidy.

But this perky little summary of my life and marriage doesn't touch on the difficulties we had getting pregnant or the tough parts of being a stepmom. It doesn't cover the struggles of coping with aging parents or losing my hearing suddenly over the course of twenty-four hours. It doesn't share Eric's cancer and the heartbreak and the inevitable bumps in the road of life. I'm still learning to be grateful for all the ups and downs because they've made me the person I am.

On the outside, I was *killing* it, and that's what the world saw. On the inside, though, I felt like I was barely holding on by a thread. But I couldn't clearly articulate what the problem was. That dichotomy between how I looked to the world and how I felt on the inside was widening.

The year and a half following Eric's birthday party would be a wild ride. While my drinking wasn't always excessive, it grew more consistent. That party wasn't my last blackout and ugly hangover experience, but it was an important milestone on my path to permanent sobriety.

3

Generation Booze

I had my first taste of alcohol at the age of fourteen, when I started hanging out with some questionable older friends. One of their grandmothers was out of town, and her loving grandson had the keys, so we threw ourselves a party. A lot of peach schnapps was involved, so the details are foggy, but a neighbor was watching the house and called the cops. My first experience with alcohol resulted in my parents having to pick me up from the police station.

After that night, I didn't start drinking regularly, but the damage was done. I would now associate alcohol with having a good time. The innocence of youth was gone. A get-together without booze suddenly seemed pointless. Now, I would equate fun with drinking and not getting caught.

I now knew how drinking felt for someone like me who was shy and struggled to fit in. With alcohol, I felt brave, outgoing, and social, and it stripped away all that awkwardness. Alcohol made me someone who could fit in and be liked. It helped me release my inhibitions and be bold in all the ways I couldn't when I was sober. Drinking seemed to soften all those blunt edges that prevented me from feeling comfortable in my own skin. Why would I want to deal with the pain of socializing sober?

College was more of the same, but our drinking there wasn't just saved for the once- or twice-a-month party in a field or the house of someone whose parents were out of town. Now we could drink whenever and wherever we wanted, and we flexed our independence muscles by doing just that. We made alcohol a part of everything we did. Fake IDs were a requirement, and beer bongs were standard issue. Keg stands, shotgunning beers, and case races were symbols of badassery.

College confirmed that I was a blackout drinker. I never puked like most of my friends. Instead, I would cross some invisible threshold, and my body just turned off. BOOM—blackout. Hours of my life could go missing while I was still totally conscious, walking around and partying. People who have never experienced it don't understand. They'll say things like, "You have to remember something!" Nope, that's not how it works. Total darkness, zero memories, *huge* risk.

For a long time, I mistakenly thought it was my generation of women who perfected the art of binge drinking. Because I was living it and seeing it all around me with women my age, it seemed like we were the ones blazing the trails. We were doing it so well. As it turns out, we were only a small part of a much larger cohort: Generation Booze.

Over the last fifty to seventy-five years, women have turned drinking into a sport, a rite of passage, and a staple of teenage and adult life. Beer and whiskey weren't just for boys anymore—we gals could hold our own in a major way. It became a symbol of women's independence. We even made it a pillar of motherhood and created a whole culture around mommies and their wine.

My mom faced similar attitudes toward drinking when she was a single flight attendant living in Miami. My younger cousin dealt with the same as she graduated from college in the past few years. There was nothing unique about my generation. We just carried the torch that we would then pass off to the next group of women.

Our society has turned heavy drinking into a norm that is commonly accepted. It has become so ingrained in our habits and routines that we don't think twice about it. We use alcohol to mark almost every life occasion, milestone, and daily event. We excel at turning just about anything on the calendar into an occasion for drinking.

Generation Booze has created a culture that glorifies and glamorizes extreme drunkenness and encourages reckless and dangerous behavior. In college, we learn that it's hilarious to get fall-down drunk and that the ability to drink large amounts of alcohol is a badge of honor. I saw friends end up in the hospital, break bones, and become victims of sexual assault—all because binge drinking was celebrated and encouraged. I can only pray that future generations will soon start taking things in the other direction.

All my thoughts about the culture of college drinking were highlighted when my family recently made the trip to my alma mater, Virginia Tech, with my best friend and her family. We spent a weekend together in Blacksburg and took our six kids to their first Hokie football game.

I've probably been to twenty-five football games in Lane Stadium since my first year of college at Virginia Tech. When I was a freshman, Michael Vick was our superstar, and ESPN Gameday was on campus every week. It was a great time to be a Hokie. I'm sure the football experience seemed fun at the time, as we drunkenly stumbled into the stadium after hours of tailgating. We often left the games early to hit the bars downtown and continue the party into the night. When I've gone back for games as an adult, drinking has been a huge part of the experience, even if it wasn't as intense as our college years. The whole day revolved around it. We would meticulously plan when to start pre-gaming, where to do it, what to drink, how we would get booze into the game, and where we could keep drinking after the game. The football game was secondary.

If you told me a few years ago that the game I would have the *most* fun at would be one when I was forty-two, with my kids, and stone-cold sober, I probably wouldn't have believed you. This time, a year into being alcohol-free, I couldn't wait to experience a football weekend with my family without booze factoring in at all. I was obsessed with being clear-headed and able to take it all in. I watched my boys as they first saw the stadium and realized how enormous it was. I saw them giggle at all the crazy college kids in their game-day war paint. I listened to them ask a hundred times when Metallica's "Enter Sandman" would be pumped through the speakers. And then I joined them, jumping on the seats when the Metallica song started blaring, and the team ran out to fireworks and sixty-thousand fans singing along and surging up and down in the bleachers. It was electric. Then we watched every minute of a fantastic Hokie win and screamed our hearts out each time the cannon blasted to signify a touchdown. The night was full of joy—and free of booze.

4

Finding My Voice

I struggled with my weight and body image for what seems like my entire life. I went on my first diet in second grade. I don't remember what it entailed, and I didn't tell my parents. I simply decided that I needed to lose weight, and I made it happen. For a while in high school, I basically stopped eating and got very thin. Thankfully, it didn't snowball into a major eating disorder, and I moved on without lasting impact. A twisted and sick part of me has looked back on that time and glamorized it, thinking it was when I was at my "perfect weight."

College brought more challenges, more fad diets, and more body dysmorphia. Regular binge drinking compounded those issues. I can't begin to count how many calories I consumed each week from alcohol and drunken late-night Gumby's pizza orders.

I was always looking for a shortcut or quick fix. Hours of cardio at the gym, Snackwells low-fat foods, Slim Fast shakes, the South Beach Diet. I didn't care what I was putting in my body as long as it somehow promised to make me skinny. I exercised sporadically, always as a punishment for what I had or hadn't eaten. I rarely felt good about what I saw in the mirror, and I wasted countless hours of my life trying to take up less space in the world.

That toxic relationship with the scale and dieting continued for years.

Once I got married and started having children, I was in a much better place, but deep down, I knew pregnancy would be like navigating a body image minefield. I gained almost sixty pounds with my first pregnancy. I craved cinnamon Pop-Tarts and Skittles while pregnant with my first, and I fully leaned into the whole idea of "eating for two." I surprised myself by bouncing back relatively quickly after Caden was born, and I managed to gain a little less the second time around.

A few months after having Bryce in June 2011, I felt like an imposter in my own body and couldn't get comfortable in my skin. The weight wasn't coming off this time, and everything about my body felt different. I knew that thirty-minute jogs on the treadmill would not cut it.

I wish I could go back and hug that post-partum Hadley. I would tell her to relax and be patient. We put such unrealistic and unfair expectations on ourselves as new mothers. Although I shouldn't have been in such a hurry, I wouldn't change a thing now. The next series of events completely transformed my life in so many ways.

One evening, as I was shuffling along on the treadmill, I saw an infomercial for a crazy-looking exercise program. A guy with rippling abs was leading people through workouts that looked harder than anything I'd ever done. I listened to him talk about the benefits of the "Insanity" program, and something clicked in my mind. I decided this was just what I needed. It was crazy, but sometimes we need a little crazy. I mentioned it to a neighbor who already had the DVDs. I pirated those bad boys and dove right in.

I headed to the basement for the brutal forty-five-minute workouts each night after getting my two-year-old and four-month-old to sleep at nine o'clock. I would sweat my face off and then run upstairs to sleep for as long as possible until Bryce woke up for a feeding. I was *so* tired, but something about checking this box each day felt important. It was hard, and I was sore, but I kept checking off the days on the calendar. In the throes of mommyhood, with two under two, this was the only thing I did for *me* each day. As a bonus, the weight was flying off. A few weeks in, I had lost all my baby weight and was on my way toward being the leanest I'd ever been. I was also developing muscle tone, which was new to me. More important than all the aesthetic benefits, I was also gaining confidence. I felt stronger and more in control, and I was incredibly motivated to keep going. I got hooked on fitness, not because of how it was making me look, but because of how it was making me feel. It was empowering, and I felt unstoppable.

As time went on, I added running back into my routine and realized that all this exercise was making me a better runner than ever. I set running goals and worked toward them, using the Insanity workouts as cross-training. Then, I started including weight training, which quickly became my jam. I was developing a genuine love of fitness for all the right reasons. I was learning how good it felt to take care of my body, how to appreciate my progress, and how to push myself in all the right ways. I set my sights on a marathon and went for it. I knocked it out of the park on my first try, coming in right under the coveted four-hour mark. I felt like an athlete for the first time in my life.

Around the same time, I started learning more about the world behind these workouts that had changed my life. I discovered I could become a fitness coach and help other women like me learn how to fall in love with fitness, build their confidence, and improve their health. As with most things in my life, when

I decided to go for it, I went *all in*. I threw myself into the world of wellness coaching with a passion that few could match. I had found my calling, and my new business thrived.

Through my role as a coach, I learned about nutrition and completely changed how I ate. I learned to eat the right amount of the right foods and to stop depriving myself and restricting my calories. I learned to love vegetables, and that carbs were *not* the enemy. I also learned that my fitness performance would improve as I improved my diet. I discovered what "healthy" really felt like. I worked hard to unlearn bad habits dating back to that first diet in second grade. Coaching taught me that the number on the scale did not determine my worth. I tapped into the whole idea of self-love and self-care, and I wanted to share those messages with as many people as possible. I worked hard as a coach for six years and loved every moment. When I decided to move on, it was simply because I felt myself being pulled in another direction. The love I had found for health and fitness would never fade.

As important as being "healthy" was to me during that time, I always made space and exceptions for alcohol. I joked about it on my social media constantly. I built my brand around being a "wine-obsessed mom of boys who loves fitness." Being healthy shouldn't mean depriving ourselves of the things we love, right? I would never suggest anyone had to cut booze to be healthy. I certainly would not give up my red wine, so I wouldn't expect it of others.

I didn't drink every day. I could go for extended periods without alcohol and did so frequently over the years. This felt like further proof that I didn't have any kind of problem. I would wake up with a horrible hangover, as I did after the '80s party, and declare I was never drinking again. That vow would last a while, but I would always return to my usual habits once the bad memories from my last drinking incident dissipated.

I claimed to have a laser focus on my health, yet I often drank one or two large glasses of wine several nights a week. On the weekends, it was more like four or five drinks if we were going somewhere, celebrating something, coping with something, or the weather was beautiful. Unfortunately, no amount of quinoa and kale will compensate for ten to fifteen drinks a week. I was not treating my body well, and it was holding me back. So much for my self-care.

And then there was the concept of self-love. I was great at preaching it, but every time I woke up after drinking too much the night before, self-loathing consumed me. This wasn't the type of person I wanted to be, and no matter how many times I said it would never happen again, somehow, it always did. It's hard to love yourself when you're hungover, drowning in shame, and experiencing a three-day depressive episode after each night out. I thought I knew what self-love was supposed to look like, but I would never embody it as long as I was still drinking. I hated myself too much.

I felt like my life and career were one big lie.

What if I'd been a health coach claiming that doing a few lines of cocaine once or twice a week was fine? A health professional who supports and glamorizes regular alcohol consumption is a total oxymoron. Alcohol is poison, literally a known carcinogen—and it has finally been determined that no amount of alcohol is safe or healthy. Our bodies are designed to reject it, even though we've been conditioned to ignore the signs and symptoms, and we continue to talk about how booze can be part of a healthy lifestyle. It's good for your heart, right? Nope, any potential benefits are entirely outweighed by the fact that it's poison, which comes with a host of negative consequences. You're better off eating a bowl of blueberries for antioxidants and resveratrol than drinking a glass of pinot noir. The studies with questionable conclusions about alcohol being "good for you" are shared online as examples of why we should keep drinking. The studies about the adverse effects of drinking, increased risk of cancer, and incidences of sexual assault, heart disease, and depression are not quite as sexy. They aren't shared with quite the same vigor on Facebook by middle-aged women.

I desperately tried to be healthy for a long time while simultaneously poisoning my body. The two practices were mutually exclusive. There was no way for me to fix what was happening in my body and my life without quitting drinking completely. I can tell you without a doubt, I'm now truly healthy, inside and out, and it feels pretty damn amazing.

5

The Year That Tried to Break Me

In the year and a half following the infamous '80s party, a series of crises pummeled me. First, the COVID pandemic hit us like a Mack truck, forcing me to figure out distance learning for a second and fourth grader while simultaneously working long hours and hustling for my business. My husband was working remotely, and like so many other families, we were trying to find a new normal. It was a lot of togetherness for a major introvert like me. *A lot.*

That April, my husband was diagnosed with throat cancer. Managing chemo and daily radiation sessions was especially challenging in a pandemic when no one could enter our quarantine bubble to help with the kids. My mom helped get us through, and I thank God every day for her.

Next, just for shits and giggles, Eric was laid off from work a week before he started treatment. I thought our world was imploding. Ultimately, his break from work allowed him to focus on his treatments without stressing about his job.

Still, it was tough to accept the job loss as a blessing at first.

We were at our lake house when he got the call. He found me downstairs and nodded for me to follow him to the bedroom to tell me the news away from the kids. I somehow sensed exactly what he was going to say, and when he told me he'd been let go, I dropped to my knees. I barely had my arms around his cancer diagnosis. That was already more than my brain could handle. What were we supposed to do without his health insurance?

I walked down to the dock afterward to call my best friend, chugging two White Claws as I sobbed to her on the phone and paced. Drinking seemed like a totally reasonable thing to do, given the circumstances.

My mind was going a mile a minute, agonizing about the combination of cancer and unemployment. I hid my tears behind my sunglasses on the boat with the kids that afternoon. How would we make it through? Would he be okay? How could I raise these boys without him? I got spun up thinking about the weird logistical details of a life alone. How would I know when to change the air filters and fertilize the lawn? Of course, I felt guilty for the strange directions of my thoughts, but I later learned what I was feeling was common. I couldn't fathom the idea of losing him in all the ways that mattered, so I detached and focused on the unimportant details. They were more tangible.

Amid all this upheaval, my grandfather was slowly dying. We did that awful thing forced on us by COVID: saying goodbye to a loved one through the window of a nursing home. We were very close, and it was heartbreaking that no one could be with him in his last few weeks to hug him or hold his hand. It gutted my mom, who had been his best friend and caretaker for years. As we were getting Eric's diagnosis and learning the details of his cancer, I couldn't bring myself to tell her and pile on more grief.

My mom and I went to clear out my grandpa's assisted living apartment a few days after his death. Eric was scheduled to hear the details of his biopsy the next day, but we knew it was cancer. I was grateful that we had to wear a mask while cleaning out the apartment because it hid my face. Without it, my mom would have known something was going on. I didn't want to taint the solemnness of our task with another tragedy, so I waited to tell her until we had all the details a few days later.

Through all of this, I frequently thought to myself, *thank God for that five o'clock glass or two of wine each night.* I depended on it to help me unwind as I watched the news and tracked how my world and the world around me were slowly coming unraveled. It kept me nice and numb.

Eric couldn't drink during treatment, but I helped myself to his share. People were bringing us dinner each night through a "meal train" signup, and many sent bottles of wine. It was much appreciated, and I usually popped the cork once I got Eric settled for the night and then watched movies with the boys. I had no energy for anything else.

He slugged through the grueling treatment regimen like a trooper. It was brutal, and he was remarkably composed and positive through it all. No one can prepare you for what it feels like to put your body through that level of trauma, nor can they prepare caretakers for how hard it is to watch your loved ones in so much pain and discomfort. It went by in a blink but also somehow dragged on painfully.

A few days before his last daily radiation treatment, we learned that Eric's parents had been the victims of an elaborate financial scam targeting older adults. It was like something out of a *Dateline* special, and they were in deep. Since Eric was bound by his radiation schedule and feeling horrible from the cumulative effects, I hopped in the car for the three-hour drive to their house to fix things as much as I could.

Once I got there, I cleared the dining room table to make a command center as I tried to get my arms around the situation.

I ran on black coffee for several days as I talked to banks, police, and phone companies. I tried to change a thousand passwords while simultaneously freezing their credit. In the evening, I'd switch from coffee to cheap white wine, hoping it would bring me back down enough to fall asleep.

It took days to uncover the extent of the scam. His parents had lost a lot of money, and the scammers had all their personal info and bank account details. It would ultimately take over a year for Eric to unwind it all and take control of their finances.

During all of this personal trauma, the world around me felt like it was spinning out of control. We were at the height of unrest over racial injustice; the election was heating up, and everyone was fighting left and right over COVID mitigation tactics and what to do about schools. People were staging protests at the school board meetings a half mile from our house. On meeting nights, there were horns honking and news choppers flying overhead for hours. Everyone was losing their minds. Pour me some freaking wine.

For the first time ever, I was drinking *every* night. Gloomy 2020 created a daily wine habit that felt necessary and well deserved—a part of my day I eagerly anticipated and relied on heavily. When it hit five o'clock, I would pour myself that first glass, take a big sip, and wait for the delicious feeling of warmth and numbness to spread through my body.

The jokes about drinking through the pandemic were endless, and the memes were flying around social media. It felt like we were all in the same boat, which made me feel better about these new habits I'd settled into. We've been conditioned to believe that alcohol is a problem solver, so it was a logical solution when the world was burning around us like a dumpster fire. Drinking is an easy answer to the problems in our lives. How else were we supposed to cope with all of this craziness?

6

The Rosé That Changed It All

Like so many, we went into 2021 thinking things would be different. This COVID thing had to be winding down, election drama would be over soon, and Eric had a clean bill of health and a sparkly new job. News of a vaccine was on the horizon, and we felt a glimmer of hope for the first time in ages.

With cautious optimism, we began planning weekends at our lake house with friends. We couldn't wait to be with our people again. We were in that brief sweet spot before the Delta and Omicron variants of COVID surged, and the spring and summer felt almost magical.

Here's the thing about the lake … It puts you in immediate vacation mode. You forget about your to-do list as soon as you're on the water with the sun on your face and the wind in your hair. Your stress disappears, and you want to relax.

We often joked that it was dangerous being there too often because when you're in "lake mode," you want to drink like you're on vacation. You know how it goes. On vacation, it suddenly seems okay to have mimosas with breakfast or to pop open a bottle of pinot grigio with lunch. You need a beer in your hand when riding on the boat or lounging on the dock. That's fine once a year, but not when it's every weekend.

Eric and I were used to keeping things in check while we were there as a family, but it was different when friends visited again. When people come for the weekend, it is a vacation for them. When they arrive, they're ready to party and get their vacation drinking on. To be clear, we were never upset about it. We were prepared to throw down with them.

That summer, we had guests almost every weekend. We drank a lot, and I began to notice a troubling pattern. We would drink too much from Friday to Sunday, and then I would feel hungover and toxic for days. On Monday, my mental health would take a nosedive. A wave of depression and anxiety would hit, and I'd feel like I was in a dark hole trying to claw my way out. I'd struggle to get through my days, to be productive, and to find joy in any of my normal activities. I would still drink wine throughout the week, which only compounded the issue. By Thursday, I would come out of the fog and feel like I was returning to myself again. But then Friday would hit, and we'd head back down to the lake to start all over again.

It took me too long to recognize this pattern and acknowledge what was happening. By August, I was restless. I felt something pulling at my heart, telling me none of this was normal. I didn't feel right, and I knew something had to change. The obvious solution felt scary, so I avoided thinking about it for as long as possible. What was I supposed to do—take a break from drinking in the middle of the summer? That was crazy, right?

I started wondering if I needed more than just a break. What if I had a legitimate problem? I realized I had to consider that possibility seriously, although I had a very naïve sense of what constituted a "problem." I thought it was all or nothing—either you're a raging drunk, or you're fine. I wasn't a raging drunk, so quitting wasn't the solution, was it? I didn't know how to make sense of it all. I only knew something was wrong, and I didn't feel good in any of the ways that counted.

One weekend in August, with all of this swirling in my head, my best friend and her family were scheduled to visit. We hadn't seen them since COVID hit, and I was beyond excited. This friend is my "ride or die." She's the person I'd call if I had a body to hide. I missed her fiercely. We had planned the weekend obsessively—the menu, the cocktails, and the sleeping arrangements for the kids. I was counting down the hours until they got there.

On Friday morning, I made the beds, finished washing towels, and prepped the appetizers. Then I got the call. Her husband was sick. Nothing major, just some cold symptoms, but in this new age of COVID, that was more than enough to ruin a weekend. We had to call the whole thing off, and we were devastated.

The boys and I got together with friends from the lake that afternoon to get everyone's minds off our ruined plans. While the kids were playing, my friend and I popped the sparkling rosé I had bought for the weekend. Two bottles later, we were still lounging in the sun, laughing, talking, and pleasantly buzzed. I knew that would be enough to hit me like a freight train the next day. Those wine headaches were getting worse; just one peril of turning forty, I assumed. With a big cup of water and some Advil on my bedside table, I fell asleep (or passed out) around eight o'clock that night, knowing I had overdone it and would regret all the "fun" in the morning.

I woke up at three in the morning with hot chills, a pounding head, and the room spinning around me. I grasped for my water and chugged down the Advil, praying it would kick in fast. I sat there in bed, staring at the ceiling, knowing I wouldn't be able to fall back to sleep. I was furious with myself because I had a long run planned for that day. Why did I keep finding myself in this situation, and why did I act as if I were helpless to stop it?

I suddenly felt like something slapped me in the face. At that moment, with perfect clarity, I realized I had the power to ensure I never felt that way again. It was like my brain, heart, and body were all suddenly in alignment. It clicked, and I knew, without a doubt, I had to stop drinking. I didn't know what it would look like or how I would do it, but I knew it was the answer. Drinking was keeping me from becoming the best version of myself, and I wanted to stop the cycle.

7

Give Me All the Lexapro

I was a psychology major in college, with dreams of being a social worker or a therapist, but at no point in my life did I ever sit back and evaluate my own mental health. I never even considered talking to a therapist or digging deeper to look at my own issues. Weirdly enough, it never even crossed my mind. I assumed I was fine, and maybe I was, for a while.

Fast forward to a year after the birth of my youngest son, and I didn't feel fine anymore. I was struggling as a new mom with two under two, and every day felt like running a marathon through Jell-O. I was tired to my bones and struggling to find joy in my daily life. I was full of inexplicable rage and constantly felt like my head was going to blow off. I was so anxious that I spent most of each day imagining all the terrible things that could happen to my babies if I weren't exceptionally cautious. I was afraid of everything, I was depressed, and I was oblivious.

I went to my obstetrician for a checkup, and when she asked how I was doing, I hesitantly mumbled something about not feeling quite like myself. Thankfully, she asked some probing questions, which I answered with a trembling lip and tears in my eyes. After listening patiently, she suggested I try a prescription for an antidepressant. My first reaction was absolute shock. It hadn't even occurred to me that I was experiencing depression and anxiety. At that moment, I quickly went from shock to realization, and thought, "*holy crap, I'm depressed!*" How had I overlooked this?

Now, let me pause for the people who will jump down my throat over our collective tendency to throw medication at problems. If that's your opinion, fine, but learn to keep it to yourself. There are many ways to address mental health issues, and medication is a valid and vital option. To end the stigma around mental health and encourage people to speak up when they need help, we need to be careful not to judge them for *how* they choose to get that help.

I was a frazzled mom of two babies, and I was falling apart at the seams. At that moment, I desperately needed an easy button. If my doctor had told me to find a therapist first, read a self-help book, or do yoga in the forest, I would have come unhinged. She gave me just what I needed at that point in time: Zoloft. The antidepressant changed my life, and I will be forever grateful. It took the edge off, silenced the rage, and helped me find the joy in my life again. It calmed my anxiety to a more manageable level. I enjoyed being a mother and a human again. It didn't take away all my problems with the flick of a wand or put me in some phony state of euphoria, but it helped me see that the delicate balance of my brain chemistry had indeed been off. After a while, I switched to Lexapro to mitigate some irritating side effects. Lexapro and I just *clicked*. We were besties, and I thought we'd never break up. I would tell anyone and everyone that I took it, and I shared about it liberally on my social media accounts. I wanted to make it "cool" to be open about mental health struggles. I wanted taking medicine for mental health to be just as accepted as taking medicine for physical health.

Was I still drinking while taking this medication? Absolutely! The guidance to not consume alcohol seemed like merely a suggestion. Everyone I knew seemed to ignore that fine print on the bottle.

Years later, 2019 rolled around. I felt a nudge telling me I was in a different place. I was happy and stable and felt very in control of my mental health. *Maybe* I didn't need my beloved Lexapro anymore. Did I really want to take this medicine for the rest of my life? I talked to my doctor, who said he would support me either way—if I decided to continue or wanted to wean myself off. There is often a period of withdrawal, and sometimes your symptoms can be exacerbated as your brain and body re-calibrate to find their new normal after medication. I did lots of reading about the process and knew what to expect. I made the thoughtful decision to experiment with life after Lexapro. I weaned myself off, although not as slowly as I should have, and it hit me like a ton of bricks.

I experienced a lot of intense depression in the months after I came off the meds. It would come in waves that knocked me on my ass. Everything I read said this was normal, and I decided to stick through it. My mantra was, "I'm not okay, but it's okay that I'm not okay." I felt strongly that once things settled down, I would be glad I had pushed through. I knew what to look out for if I ever needed to go back on medication down the road. I would never again stick my head in the sand and ignore my mental health. I told myself I'd be fine with it if I ultimately determined I needed to stay on meds forever, but I was determined to give it a shot and see if I could go without.

Toward the end of 2019, after months of ups and downs, I finally felt myself settling into a comfortable space. I had occasional bad days, but no more of the heavy depressive episodes that had been plaguing me. I was, for the most part, happy, content, and glad I had pushed through and come off the medication.

I was feeling very smug about my new, un-medicated self, out there crushing it in the world. I hit my stride in the first few months of 2020. My family was doing well, I was thriving, and my fitness coaching business was on the upswing. Life was *good*. I felt stable and strong.

You already know how this story goes. We started hearing about this virus called COVID-19, and the news just kept getting worse. Life suddenly felt strange and uncertain, but I was hanging in there and proud of myself for handling things so well. Over the next few months, as we were bombarded with curveballs—the cancer diagnosis, my grandfather's death, Eric's layoff, and what appeared to be permanent distance learning for the kids—I realized it was too much, and I didn't feel okay anymore. My anxiety level rose, and I struggled to make it through each day. There was so much uncertainty, countless hard decisions to make, and so much fear for the future. That five o'clock glass of wine was no longer enough to do the trick.

I quickly decided I did not need to be some kind of hero by trying to raw dog it through this epic pile of crap life had heaped on our doorstep. I knew I needed to be as healthy, mentally and physically, as I could be to get my family through these challenges.

I called my doctor and said, "Give me all the Lexapro!"

I knew I had to keep myself from slipping back into that dark place, and I was *so* glad I didn't waste any time debating it. For a split second, I was frustrated that I had seemingly wasted a year weaning myself off only to jump right back on the Lexapro bandwagon, but I didn't let myself dwell on it. These were crazy, unprecedented times, and it was all about survival.

Going back on that medication was the right decision, and I

was grateful for that pharmacological support as I navigated one of the most challenging years of my life. Once I made it to the other side, I decided I had no interest in messing with a good thing. Even though my life situation had improved, and I was feeling better, you would now have to pry the Lexapro out of my cold, dead hands.

I was in a mostly stable place with my mental health until the summer of 2021, when my drinking escalated, and I started noticing those distinct patterns around my depressive episodes and weekend binge drinking. This pattern was a big part of what ultimately led me to make a change.

You're not supposed to drink while on antidepressants or SSRIs. I was creating a mental health shitstorm for myself. Alcohol itself exacerbates anxiety and depression, and I was essentially negating the effects of my medication while making my mental state even worse.

When I walked away from booze for good, I saw almost immediate improvement. Once the alcohol was flushed from my system, it brought me right back to that stable, content, happy place. It felt like I had shed an unnecessary layer of depression, *and* I was allowing my medicine to do its essential job once again. It was empowering to realize I could pull that lever and make such a positive change for my life and well-being. It was also a little disturbing that I had let things go for as long as I had.

While eliminating alcohol is not an immediate cure for our mental health struggles, it can have a tremendous impact. It certainly did for me. I'm not suggesting I'll never again face issues. Life will not always be sunshine and daisies. That's unrealistic and naïve. I do feel content and at peace knowing that any future ups and downs that I'll inevitably face will not be further fueled by booze.

8

The Lady in the Red Car

One day, many years ago, I was heading to my hot yoga class to sweat my face off and purge the glass of wine I'd likely had the night before. I was early, so I ran into the grocery store to grab something. While I waited in the checkout line, a disheveled-looking woman came flying past in a whirlwind. She cut in front of me and put her single purchase on the belt in front of the cashier without even acknowledging me. I was so stunned that I couldn't form the words to call her out. As I stood there gawking, I realized her one item was a four-pack of those mini bottles of wine—the six-ounce bottles you buy for cooking. I took a deep breath and reminded myself to give her the benefit of the doubt. Maybe she was a frazzled chef, and this was an early-morning chicken marsala *emergency*.

    Once I made my purchase and headed to my car, I happened to look over and see that same woman sitting in a beat-up red car a few spots down. She was sitting in the driver's seat, chugging those little bottles of wine, one right after the other—the equivalent of an entire bottle. She tossed the last bottle over her shoulder, threw the car into drive, and sped out of the parking lot like a scene from a movie. I sat there, stunned, with my mind racing. What if she hurt herself or someone else? I called the police, but I hadn't gotten her plate number, and it was too late for them to track her down.

The whole thing gave me knots in my stomach, but I couldn't articulate why. Maybe it's because I had never witnessed that kind of drinking before. I was blessed not to have a front-row seat to that type of pain and struggle. It was something you read about in books, but I'd never experienced it in my personal bubble.

I often thought back to that woman as I sifted through my relationship with alcohol in the two years before I called it quits. I knew something about my drinking didn't feel right, but I wasn't disheveled and chugging wine in the grocery store parking lot. Something still felt off, though, and I didn't know how to reconcile that.

I thought my problem had to look like her problem for me to do something about it. I would read through the online checklists and say, "I don't drink in secret or first thing in the morning. I don't drive drunk." I didn't check all the boxes, so I thought that meant I didn't have a problem and shouldn't have to change anything. But if I didn't technically have a "problem," then why did I still feel so off? How was alcohol having such a clear impact on my mental and physical health?

After letting all of this brew in my mind and heart for that one miserable summer, my middle-of-the-night epiphany at the lake made so many things clear. It didn't matter if I looked anything like the woman in the red car. What mattered was that alcohol had become a big problem for me. It was, without a doubt, having a negative impact on my life. I realized I didn't need to meet anyone's definition but my own to make the change I knew I needed. As I started to accept and explore all of this, I learned that Alcohol Use Disorder rarely looks like the extreme images we conjure up in our minds. It's not always the unkempt person stumbling around with a bottle supposedly hidden in a brown paper bag. It's often the mom you see at the bus stop who looks perfectly put together, or it's the guy from work you eat lunch with every day but have no idea he's struggling. It's that college friend who looks like they have the perfect family and life on Instagram. We think we're the only ones experiencing issues, but we're not. Statistically, we're everywhere.

Just because we haven't crashed our cars and don't need to be shipped off to rehab immediately doesn't mean we can't still drastically improve our quality of life. Contrary to popular belief, rock bottom is not a required step in the process. We simply have to learn to ask ourselves the right questions to get started instead of blindly following old, misguided ideas about alcohol that have been perpetuated for years.

Think about the questions you might have asked yourself and decide whether they're the right ones. If you're hung up on the old standard, "Am I an alcoholic?" it could hold you back. Try asking yourself these today and really pay attention to how you feel as you answer them:

Do you feel that alcohol is making your life worse instead of better?

Do you feel like drinking is holding you back from your best life?

Do you feel like it's taking more than it's giving?

Does your gut tell you that alcohol is causing you problems?

Clear your mind of the stereotypes of what someone with a problem looks like, and really think about how you feel. Is something off in the balance of your life?

Alcohol told me a lot of big fat lies before I realized what an asshole it was. It was like the high school boyfriend who was hot and popular, and you wanted him to be perfect, so even when you started realizing what a douche canoe he was, you kept pretending he was great, because breaking up might affect your social life. Alcohol promised to make me outgoing and sexy. It promised to make me funny, charismatic, and popular. It promised to help me handle stress and the demands of life and motherhood. It promised to make life fun, glamorous, and easy.

Alcohol was full of shit.

It made me anxious, depressed, bloated, and miserable. It filled me with shame and regret. It held me back from reaching my potential. If it had been a man making me feel those things, I would have dumped his ass twenty-five years ago. Instead, I stayed in that toxic relationship for decades too long and allowed the abuse to continue.

Lately, I've wondered about that woman in the red car. I hope she's okay, and I hope she's figured out some of these same lessons for herself. I pray she's not still stuck in that same cycle because no one deserves that. We all deserve so much more than a life limited by the messy grasp of alcohol.

9

"I QUIT"

When I woke up at three in the morning after drinking that fateful bottle of rosé with what I decided would be my last hangover, I knew I had a big challenge ahead. The first step was owning my problem. I didn't know or care if my problem was worthy of any "official" label, but it was a problem for me, and that was enough.

I still don't relate to the term "alcoholic," and it's not because I'm in denial. I don't like the way the word is weaponized or the idea that once someone is labeled that way, they're stuck with it for life, like an incurable disease. I understand the concept and the rationale, and I get that it's an integral part of the Alcoholics Anonymous vernacular, but it just doesn't feel right to me. The key words here are "to me." AA and all that goes along with it is a blessing for many, and I'm not discounting that.

Despite the frequency with which we hear them, the terms "alcoholic" and "alcoholism" are more colloquial and are not, in fact, medical terms or diagnoses. "Alcohol Use Disorder" or AUD is the more appropriate terminology, and it accurately reflects that problems occur on a spectrum, ranging from mild to severe. It's not binary, it's not simple, and no checklist will be perfect. The term "alcoholic" promotes the misguided idea that people fall into two categories. Either you're an alcoholic, or you're "normal," and you don't have a problem. The term imparts a stigma that keeps many people from addressing their relationship with alcohol. They ignore their problems because, like me, they don't check the boxes on the online questionnaires and don't want to be associated with all the negative connotations.

It shouldn't matter if you drink once a month, once a day, or you're at some tragic version of rock bottom. If alcohol is creating problems and holding you back from living fully, you can quit anytime. Depending on where you fall on the AUD spectrum, it may be considerably more difficult, but it can be done with the proper support. Quitting doesn't mean you're weak. It doesn't mean you're a failure. It doesn't mean you're less than worthy. It means you're brave and strong as hell.

I fell more into the category of "Gray Area Drinking." This is a newer term coined by Jolene Park in her 2017 Tedx Talk.[1] It's often used to describe people who consume more than a moderate amount of alcohol but don't quite meet the criteria for dependence. I was hanging out somewhere on that spectrum.

But where I fell doesn't make a difference.

My mental health was suffering; I was depressed, anxious, and drowning in shame. Hangovers were kicking my ass, and I was miserable. I wanted *off* the hamster wheel. I knew it wouldn't be easy, but I knew in my bones that I was doing the right thing, which made it easier to push forward.

Acknowledging that my relationship with alcohol was problematic finally helped me unpack the truth about our messy, ongoing love affair. For every cozy glass of red wine with a book by the fire, there were many mornings full of shame and regret. For every refreshing beer on a hot day with friends, there were just as many miserable Sundays spent wasting away on the couch. For every party where I let loose and (supposedly) had a blast, there were hours spent agonizing over missing memories and wondering if I did or said anything unforgivable. For every situation where a few cocktails made me feel bold and sexy, there were days after when I was anxious and depressed.

Sitting there in my bed at three in the morning with the spins, I decided to start with a seventy-five-day wellness challenge I had been considering, called 75 Hard. One requirement of the program is that you eliminate drinking, and this felt like a good start for me because it gave me a reason not to drink. It gave me an alibi. It also gave me some structure and a daily checklist to focus on. That's where I thrive, and I knew it would get me off to a good start. It felt scary to say I was quitting for good, so this felt like a compromise I could get my arms around.

There's a lot of buzz about 75 Hard on social media, and some consider it extreme and unsustainable. I'm not suggesting the challenge as a replicable approach to sobriety, but it was just what I needed. The exercise and nutrition components already fit with my lifestyle, so I wasn't making a lot of significant changes at once.

I finally fell back asleep, knowing I'd have to struggle through one last day of feeling like crap but also knowing things would get better. I woke up later in the morning with the hangover I was expecting, along with a fresh supply of hope, resolve, and confidence.

Not even a week into my seventy-five-day challenge, I felt like a new person. I could feel the fog lifting. Part of it was the physical boost from eliminating alcohol, but part was a mental boost just from knowing I was doing something so necessary. I blinked, and a week turned into a month, one month turned into two, and before I knew it, my seventy-five days were up. I loved hitting that daily button on my checklist for "no alcohol." Each day, I felt like I was adding a little joy back into my life.

I was returning to myself and who I was supposed to be. Long before the challenge was up, something clicked. I realized this would be it for me—I wasn't going back. Those first seventy-five days were going to be the beginning of the rest of my life, and I couldn't wait to keep going.

I'm not saying it was easy, that there weren't ups and downs and times I wanted to give up and drink my face off. It wasn't all sunshine and roses. Even when it was hard, though, I knew it was worth it. That little voice in my heart kept whispering that I was on the right path. The challenging parts of not drinking were infinitely more manageable than actually drinking and all that went with it.

I didn't go to AA. I didn't need rehab. I didn't have to detox or go through any withdrawal worse than a one-day hangover. I did no traditional recovery programs. Those approaches are a hundred and fifty percent valid and help many people, but I didn't relate to them or feel the need. I was blessed with the ability to decide I needed to stop drinking and then run with it. Annie Grace, the author of *This Naked Mind: Control Alcohol, Find Freedom, Discover Happiness, and Change Your Life*, refers to it as *spontaneous sobriety*.[2]

I finally paid attention to the red flags I had ignored for so long. I realized I would be better off without alcohol, and I went all in on my decision. Pulling the plug on booze didn't magically solve all my problems, but it allowed the smoke to clear from the pockets of wreckage in my life so I could focus on them and fix them properly.

I made myself look at my reflection in the mirror and be very honest about who I was and who I wanted to be. I had to admit that drinking was the reason for the delta between the two. I tried to stay unbiased in my assessment of my drinking habits and the issues I now realized stemmed from them. I committed to putting in the hard work as I gently guided myself through the process.

I devoured "Quit Lit" books to learn from others' experiences, which was probably the most influential factor in my early sobriety. (Quit Lit is a genre of sobriety books about quitting drinking, getting sober, and life without alcohol.) I probably read ten books in the first two months after my three-a.m. wake-up call. They were like chocolate for my soul. They filled me up and kept me going, and I *knew* I could do this when I had examples of so many others doing it before me. It helped to know I wasn't alone in all of this. I'd give anything for the chance to have a dinner party with all of these sober authors at one table. We would drink gallons of sparkling water and laugh until we cried while exchanging deep and meaningful insights from our life experiences.

Reading also taught me about the physical effects of drinking, alcohol's impact on the brain, and its increasingly glaring links to cancer. Arming myself with information was key to staying motivated. The science is clear—alcohol is poison, and no amount is healthy. Once you know that, it's hard to imagine going back.

I listened to podcasts and plugged into the incredibly supportive sobriety communities on Instagram and Facebook. I realized how many of us are out there and how important connection is during this process.

I took care of myself aggressively. I allowed myself to rest and sleep a lot, exercise a ton, and eat well. I went for walks, tried meditating, and let myself feel all the feelings.

I also talked about it a lot. I wrote about my decision and shared it on social media. I told my friends and family, perhaps way more than they wanted to hear.

I allowed myself to be selfish for a while, treating myself with kid gloves while I figured it all out. Some days were beautiful;

some days were messy and raw. That's what being a human is all about, though—balancing that fine line between beauty and mess.

Education, community, and self-care were the three pillars of my sobriety, like the three legs of a stool. I needed each of them to keep me upright, and they worked together beautifully. There was nothing magical about my process. I kept reminding myself that alcohol-free Hadley felt amazing, and I never wanted to go back.

There were still triggers to work through, and that may always be the case. I may occasionally think about wine at five o'clock sharp or yearn for a margarita on a sunny day before realizing it doesn't actually seem at all appealing anymore. There may still be times when I feel frustrated, jealous, or angry that I don't get to drink in certain situations. I may always have drinking dreams that wake me up in a cold sweat and leave a pit in my stomach.

It gets easier, though, I promise. It's liberating when you wake up one day and realize you don't miss it, you don't crave it, and you feel lucky to be free of it.

The biggest struggle for me, early on, was each evening when I started dinner. That had typically been my daily opportunity to open the wine bottle and "unwind" before the craziness with the kids set in. I got a little twitchy each day as I tried to ignore that trigger and push through, so I found a way to acknowledge it and give myself a little tender loving care along the way. At five o'clock sharp, I would make myself a cup of herbal tea or pour some kombucha. I would grab my book and head into our sunroom alone and give myself fifteen minutes to read and sip my drink in peace. It was like a mental reset before I even thought about dinner or evening activities, and it made a huge difference. The habit stuck, and I still look forward to my five o'clock quiet time each day. I turned my evening wine habit into an evening self-care routine that still keeps me sane.

I've also been through lots of "firsts," which will probably continue for years. I've been to my first party as the only sober person, my first girls' night, concert, and my first sober vacation. Someday, I'll have my first sober wedding to attend or my first sober trip to Italy or France. As I experience each "first," I build my confidence and grow stronger. I have learned to find joy in the journey, and it's shaping me into the person I've always known I wanted to be.

My less-than-traditional, self-designed route to recovery will certainly not work for all. There are countless options out there, and I encourage you to ask for help and find something that works for you. It's so important to get the support you need. I can say definitively that no form of recovery is more valid than another. We're all different people with unique issues, backgrounds, and personalities. There is no cookie-cutter approach to sobriety, so never let someone tell you there is. Sometimes it takes more than one try, and sometimes it takes more than one approach. The important thing is to keep trying.

10

Thinking About Change with an Open Mind

As humans, we're naturally resistant to change. We dig our heels in and do our best to maintain the status quo, even if it's hurting us. Change feels scary. It's much easier to stick our heads in the sand and ignore our problems than to reach toward the sun and do the hard work that goes along with growing and evolving.

Chances are, if you've made it this far, you relate to at least *something* I've talked about. I'd love for my experience to help you make an honest evaluation of your life and habits and determine whether changing your relationship with alcohol might be as beneficial for you as it was for me. The goal is to get you excited to make that change if you decide it's necessary. Let's be clear; no one can decide for you. It has to be all *you*.

For almost two years before I finally quit drinking, I would not sit with myself in the quiet and evaluate what was happening in my life. I turned a blind eye to how I felt and refused to admit that all signs pointed to alcohol as the culprit. When I was finally forced to acknowledge the red flags practically flying in my face, I only wished that someone had helped me recognize them sooner.

I eventually got to a point where I was thrilled with the prospect of making a change. Whether or not you reach that same conclusion, the goal is to peel back your own layers and take an honest look at your life. I hope I can help you skip those two messy years I spent figuring it all out for myself!

My husband is famous for saying, "Don't complain about it if you're not willing to *do* something about it." Usually, he's saying that as I bitch about a family issue. This is what I was doing on a larger scale with my whole life back before I tackled my drinking. I was complaining (at least to myself) about all the problems I was having. I was miserable, and there was a clear solution, but I wasn't ready to acknowledge it. I didn't have an open mind about what the possible solutions might look like. I didn't want to challenge the status quo. It was easier to stick with what I knew and what was comfortable, even if "comfortable" was a hungover mess.

Despite going through week after week, incident after incident, where my drinking was causing me issues, I kept my focus narrow and refused to consider that I could lead a life that looked very different from the one I was muddling through. I was stubborn and dug my heels in like a champ.

Finally, during that last summer, riddled with hangovers, shame, and bouts of depression, I felt something in my heart opening up. I imagined a life where I didn't feel like alcohol controlled me. I thought about a life where I didn't limp from drinking episode to drinking episode. I dreamed about a life where everything didn't revolve around running for the bottle opener as soon as the clock struck five. It felt like a huge step to consider a different life than the one in which alcohol had played such an important role for so long. I started to believe that a different life might feel a hell of a lot better than my current one, but I first had to open my mind to imagine a different reality.

To make meaningful change, we have to consciously open our minds and think outside our current circumstances. We have to consider that we might need to make some hard changes to move forward and become the people we were meant to be. Life might need to look different than it does right now. It might feel tough for a while, and it might be a little scary. All of that change might lead to something beautiful and unexpected.

Right now, I encourage you to find a quiet spot, close your eyes, take a few deep breaths, and think about your life. What struggles are you dealing with? Are you wrestling with your relationship with alcohol and trying to determine how far its tentacles are reaching into your life? Have you actually opened your mind and heart to the fact that you may need to make some changes? Have you thought about what those changes might need to look like? Have you considered the implications, even if they feel messy and complicated? Are you willing to explore the options and try something new?

If you make it through this book, and if a lightbulb goes off and you decide, "WOW—there are so many signs in my life that alcohol is causing me problems!" is your mind open enough to consider making changes and steering your life in another direction? Or will you shut it down and return to the status quo?

Maybe, like me, you need some more time to get to that point, and that's fine. Or maybe taking time to consciously open your heart and mind before starting this process will make all the difference.

11

Imposter Syndrome

As I waded through the early months of life without booze, it occurred to me that maybe I had a responsibility to share my story. Could I show people a different path? Could I demonstrate that how someone looks on the outside is not an indication of what's happening on the inside? I decided to share my experience on social media. It took some courage, but the response was positive and overwhelming. *Phew!*

Soon, a startup in Australia asked me to become a "*sobriety guide*" for a new sobriety app. The app aimed to provide a fresh approach for people looking to change their relationship with alcohol. No judgment, no labels, just a place to learn from the life experiences of people who have walked that path before and come out on the other side. I immediately agreed to be a part of it, and I committed to creating two courses. Then I started to sweat. Did I actually have what it took to create valuable content for the platform?

I also felt like a sobriety fraud. I was concerned that I wasn't a good enough writer, but also that I wasn't a good enough drunk. The doubts flooded in. After all, I wasn't a "real" addict, was I? Maybe I didn't have enough of a drinking problem. After all, I'd never been through a traditional recovery program. I feared I was in no way qualified to do this and wondered if I should back out so I didn't mislead anyone.

I had a major case of "imposter syndrome."

Imposter syndrome is defined as *feelings of inadequacy that persist despite evident success*. "Imposters" suffer from self-doubt and a sense of illegitimacy that override any feelings of success or external proof of their competence.

I've felt this more times than I can count. When I worked to advance my corporate career, I worried I wasn't good enough. When I became a mother, I worried I was inadequate. When I trained for my first marathon, I doubted whether I could be successful. When I started my coaching business, I was convinced I wouldn't have what it took. When I started writing, I doubted whether I could create a product worth releasing into the world.

I think women are more susceptible to imposter syndrome. Why do we do this to ourselves? We doubt ourselves and our worth at every turn and convince ourselves that we're inadequate despite ample evidence of our many talents and successes. We try to talk ourselves out of each new venture or opportunity because we're afraid we'll fail. It has taken a lot of inner work for me to recognize when I'm doing this and talk myself off the imposter syndrome ledge. I now know that my initial reaction to just about everything will be, "*Nope!* Hadley, you aren't good enough to accomplish that." Then, I have to remind my inner critic that I can do just about anything I put my mind to.

In the past, when I'd feel the doubt creep in and I'd wonder if I was good enough, I'd muddle through and bury my feelings until it was time for my evening wine. As I took my first few sips, I'd feel that warm sense of artificial confidence spread through my body, and I'd forget my concerns for a while. I wasn't addressing the problem or doing the inner work to build self-belief. I was simply kicking the can down the road to deal with it another day. As a result, the waves of imposter syndrome were constant because I was never working to overcome them.

By far, the strangest bout of imposter syndrome I've ever experienced was related to my sobriety as I became more vocal and shared my experiences. As I opened up on social media about my choice to embrace sobriety and considered writing a book, my immediate thought was, "I'm not a *real* writer. Who the hell would read what I have to say?"

Fortunately, I caught what was happening with my thought patterns and reined them in. I laughed at myself when I realized I was trying to convince myself that my issues with drinking were not severe enough to be valid, like I was incompetent in my drunkenness *and* my sobriety, as though I needed to be sipping from a brown paper bag with breakfast or have spiraled into the pit of despair for my story to matter.

Now that I can no longer rely on alcohol to ease the burden when I doubt myself and my capabilities, I have to be extremely intentional about how I approach situations where imposter syndrome is likely to occur. I work continuously to build my confidence, like a muscle that needs to be exercised regularly.

When I questioned my ability to provide value on the sobriety app and wondered if I was qualified enough to create valuable content, I had to step back and take a deep breath. I acted as my own hype girl—I looked in the mirror and reminded myself that my words are powerful and can make a difference in people's lives. This is the kind of challenge I live for, and I decided I was going to knock it out of the park. That was the key; I made an actual *decision* to believe in myself and to go for it. I decided I would be the best damn sobriety guide I could be.

The fact that my drinking was problematic and that I realized it before things got worse is a huge win. That I took the steps necessary to quit on my own is even more significant. That makes me worthy and qualified to share my story with the world. Sometimes I feel imposter syndrome trying to sneak back in, and I have to take a step back and consciously silence that voice. My problems were valid, my experiences were legitimate, and my story is relatable. I am *one hundred percent* qualified to share it with the world, hoping it will reach even one person out there who is also struggling with alcohol. My content has reached thousands of people looking for help, and I hope this book will touch even more. Imposter syndrome has no place here—I have important things to say.

Are there places in your life where imposter syndrome haunts you, trying to convince you to play small? If so, I urge you to acknowledge that voice and its negativity, but then rise above it. Look at yourself in the mirror and remind yourself that you're capable of so much greatness. Don't let your mind trick you into limiting yourself, when deep down you know you are limitless.

12

What the Hell is Moderation?

There are lots of annoying things you'll hear when you stop drinking, but my absolute favorite is, "Why don't you drink in moderation instead of quitting?" THANKS, BOB! WOW! I never thought of that!

Moderation is a sensitive subject when it comes to drinking, and it looks a little different for everyone. Here is what moderation looks like for my husband, who I refer to as a moderation unicorn: He enjoys good bourbon. He likes a beer now and then or a glass of red wine occasionally. He has a drink several times a week if the opportunity presents itself, but he doesn't stress over it either way. He might go long stretches without it, and it doesn't even cross his mind. He doesn't worry about whether he'll have a drink each night or how many he'll have. He doesn't make crazy rules for himself and his drinking. He spends virtually no mental energy on thoughts of drinking. It sounds easy, and for him, it is. He drinks moderately and doesn't give it a second thought.

Now, here is what my attempts at moderation looked like: I would drink too much and end up with a hangover that prompted me to declare that I was never drinking again. I would take a break from drinking and go a week or two with no alcohol. I'd make a big stink about how I was only going to drink in moderation from now on. For the first week, I would stick to my limits. Then the weekend would roll around, and I'd slip into my old patterns, get wasted, and maybe even black out because I was drinking so fast. I'd get mad at myself and feel ashamed, so I would make new rules—no more wine on weeknights and no more than three drinks on the weekends. Then I would realize there was an open bottle of my favorite wine in the fridge. I should finish that first so it doesn't go to waste. Then I could cut out weeknights. Every night I'd agonize over whether it could be a drinking night. I'd negotiate with myself to change the rules. Once my inhibitions were lowered, I stopped caring. Then the shame would make a repeat appearance. It was like a roller coaster I rode for more than twenty-five years. Drink too much, try to rein it in, take a break for a while, slowly fall into my old habits, make a bunch of rules, break all the rules, feel ashamed. Wash, rinse, repeat.

It was *never* easy, and I always spent incredible mental energy agonizing over this cycle. The concept of moderation was always just out of reach. Have you ever taken kids bowling with the lane bumpers up? The kiddos are trying to get the ball down the middle, but it keeps bouncing from one bumper to the other. That was me, trying to drink moderately. Bouncing off the sides and never making it in a straight line down the middle.

We're inundated with messages implying that if we can't moderate, we're weak. It seems backward to me now that there's a stigma around not being able to moderate an addictive substance. Alcohol's very nature makes it difficult to moderate. In fact, it's the only drug we've determined is okay in moderation. Think about how strange that is. No one would say it's okay to smoke in moderation or that crystal meth is fine as long as it's only on special occasions. Yet, we all seem to accept the idea that we should be able to drink moderately.

Is there any actual guidance sharing what constitutes "moderate drinking?" Well, the CDC website says the following: "To reduce the risk of alcohol-related harms, the 2020-2025 Dietary Guidelines for Americans recommends that adults of legal drinking age can choose not to drink, or to drink in moderation by limiting intake to 2 drinks or less in a day for men or 1 drink or less in a day for women, on days when alcohol is consumed."[1]

When I hear people talking about drinking moderately, I don't think they're referring to any specific guidelines. Most people use this word ambiguously and don't even know how they're defining it.

I'll give you my personal definition that may help make sense of things. Moderation is the ability to limit your intake to a reasonable amount *without* stressing and agonizing over that limit, beating yourself up to stay within it, or creating rules and making exceptions constantly. It's being able to take it or leave it, expending no stress and no extra mental energy over the maintenance of said moderation. In other words, it's having a few drinks when you want them without constantly thinking and stressing about them.

Moderation isn't black and white, and not everyone can manage or regulate it in the same way. It's not as cut and dry as people try to make it out to be. The ability to moderate is a combination of nature and nurture. It's a skill or proclivity that some people seem to be naturally predisposed to. We should not be judged or feel shame if we can't moderate our consumption of a highly addictive substance.

Moderation failed me over and over, and I was ashamed I couldn't figure it out. It wasn't until I was forty-one that I finally said, "*Wait*! If moderation doesn't work for me, I can accept that and move on. I can remove moderation from my toolbox because it's not actually a tool, and I can figure out what will work."

For me, it was liberating to release the concept of moderation and discover that it took far less stress and energy to quit drinking than it did to continually chase the idea of moderation.

If you've struggled with this concept, think about which example of moderation you relate to the most. My husband's version or mine?

Think about these questions to help guide you:

Do you create rules around your drinking?

Do you think each day about whether or not to drink?

Do you negotiate with yourself or rationalize your choices?

Do you constantly feel you're starting over in your efforts to moderate?

Do you spend a significant amount of mental energy deciding when and how much to drink?

Do you feel shame about your struggle to find moderation?

Does it feel really easy, or does it feel hard?

If you answered yes to even a few of those questions, it might be a sign that moderation doesn't work for you, either. There is *absolutely nothing wrong with that*, no matter how much we've been conditioned to think it should be easy. I am a strong, independent, intelligent, and capable woman … and moderating never felt easy to me for a single day. If I asked my husband if it felt easy, it would confuse him because he's never even had to give it much thought. See the difference?

I spent a lot of time trying to make moderation work, and while I was focused on that, it was holding me back. I was convinced that keeping alcohol in my life was necessary, and moderation was the answer. Beating my head against the moderation wall kept me from pursuing more effective options that could have affected a real change in my life. As long as we're hung up on the idea that moderation is *supposed* to work for us, we're missing out on the things that might actually work.

You know what they say—the definition of insanity is doing the same thing over and over and expecting a different result. I'd been doing the same thing over and over for nearly three decades without success, so if moderation was no longer an option, I had to find another alternative. Something had to give.

When I broke it down, it seemed like there were only three logical choices. Either I could:

Drink myself into oblivion and dive off the cliff into a more severe drinking problem.

Continue to desperately and painfully grapple with this ridiculous notion of moderation that clearly didn't work.

Or, finally, quit drinking entirely and leave all those issues behind.

Thinking of my choices this way was enlightening. When I looked at them, only one option made any sense. I finally opened my mind and heart to acknowledge that not drinking at all was the right option for me.

I know those three choices might sound oversimplified, but what other options were there? It was so empowering to accept this. I'm not suggesting it was an easy decision, but it felt like the choice that made the most sense, and I worked to become at peace with it.

Suddenly, I didn't feel like a failure because I couldn't master moderate drinking. I felt like I was stepping into my power by realizing and accepting that it just didn't work for me. Instead of trying and failing repeatedly, I was choosing a new option I knew *would* work.

I still had to learn to walk the path through sobriety, but it was less work than constantly trying and failing at moderation. I saw a quote on Instagram of unknown origin that summarized my feelings perfectly: "It takes more energy to try to control your alcohol intake than it does to let go of alcohol for good." That is precisely how I felt. Suddenly, I had *one* task to worry about (DON'T DRINK AT ALL) instead of fighting this constant internal battle over when/how much/how many/how often. It was an incredible relief.

If moderation doesn't work for you either, you still have work to do. Figure out what support you need to change your relationship with alcohol and do it in a way that works for you. Acknowledging and accepting that moderation is off the menu is a powerful first step because it's so tempting to continue grappling with it.

Consider creating an affirmation to help with this idea—something you can repeat with conviction each morning or in those moments when you doubt yourself. It can keep you strong when you find yourself wondering if maybe *now* is your time to finally master moderation. The uncomfortable truth is: If you haven't mastered it yet, you likely won't.

Here is my affirmation, and you can build from it: "I am strong, capable, intelligent, worthy, and resilient. I am honoring myself by accepting that moderation is *not* my jam. I am releasing myself from the idea that I should be able to drink moderately and stepping into my power by choosing an alcohol-free life. This is not a failure; this is the ultimate success."

Your affirmation should reinforce the idea that you're releasing moderation as a strategy. Remind yourself often that alcohol, by nature, is difficult to moderate. It's an addictive substance, so if we don't feel good about moderating, it makes sense to avoid it altogether.

If you've spent even a fraction of the time I did trying to moderate my drinking … it's time to accept that it's never going to happen. Let it go. You will not wake up one morning and magically figure it out. I wish someone had told me that sooner so I could have saved myself all the effort.

13

Sharing is Scary

It's scary to share about struggles with alcohol. You feel raw and vulnerable and open to all kinds of judgment. People can be supportive, uplifting, and beautiful, but they can also be ugly and unkind, especially on the internet. You must believe your message has the power to help people, and that power transcends the opinions of cyber bullies hiding behind their screens like cowards.

When I started writing, I told myself it would only be for me. I knew getting all these thoughts out would help me process my experience. I started sharing little tidbits of my journey on social media, and the reaction surprised me. People were receptive, they seemed to relate, and many were reaching out privately. They were asking for more. They were commiserating. This struggle I'd been dealing with quietly, I wasn't the only one dealing with it. I wasn't alone.

At first, I thought I'd just keep trickling out little tidbits on social media. I was concerned about oversharing. What if my son's teacher saw my post, or our pastor, or one of my cousins? Would the other moms think I'd been hiding a bottle of chardonnay in my purse at PTA meetings or soccer games? (I admit I sneaked a bottle of wine into a swim meet once, but that's another story.)

As I was writing about my experience, I was devouring books by women talking about their own experiences with alcohol and the ups and downs of choosing sobriety. These books gave me strength and clarity, but they also opened my eyes to how damn brave it is to share like that. I read as these incredible women bared their souls and opened up about their rock-bottom moments. They talked about the impact drinking had on their lives, children, and marriages. They spoke of moments where they could have lost it all and moments when they actually did. They were vulnerable and courageous because they knew their story would be an invaluable map for someone else starting their own journey. They were walking ahead on the path and holding a light for the rest of us.

While reading their stories, I had a lightning-bolt moment. It was time for me to share my own truths, even if it felt big and scary. Enough people had reached out in response to my posts that I knew I was on to something. My story differed from those in the books I was reading, and I knew it would touch different people.

The authors I read had hit their own version of rock bottom. Some were drinking entire bottles of vodka every day and hiding booze all over the house. Some were getting DUIs, and others were losing their jobs, their marriages, and their kids. They were deep in the throes of addiction. I didn't see myself in their stories. I was inspired but never had that moment of, "*Yes*, that's exactly how I feel!" I felt slightly disconnected from their experiences because they weren't like mine.

My drinking had not taken me to that point—yet. Did I have a drinking problem? Yes. Was my life on the verge of imploding? No. We were all on the Alcohol Use Disorder spectrum, just at very different places.

No one with less extreme problems, like mine, was talking about the issues stemming from their drinking. I couldn't find anyone who was sharing the challenges of alcohol from that perspective. I could find plenty of stories about what happened once you hit rock bottom, but none telling you how to keep from getting there in the first place. Someone needed to share that perspective, I figured, and that would be me. Since then, several incredible books have come to fill this important space, and that's a huge win for all of us.

I wanted to give hope to women who felt like something was "off" but were too afraid to fully acknowledge and confront the problem. I wanted to help women who didn't realize that quitting could drastically change their lives for the better, even if their issues with alcohol seemed minor. I wanted to show that alcoholism is not binary—either you have it or you don't. Alcohol Use Disorder is much more nuanced than that. I wanted to fight the stigma around the labels and old vernacular and help people understand that problems with drinking don't have a certain look.

I decided I didn't care if it shocked Mary from the PTA to hear that I blacked out at a winery or drank too much White Claw at the lake. I'd rather be real and raw and honest with a chance that my story might help someone than push it all down inside so I don't ruffle any feathers. I'd rather my experiences had a purpose—all the hangovers, shame, regret, and the mornings spent swearing I'd never drink again. I'd rather know it was all just fuel for this next stage of my life, where I would turn that pain into something beautiful.

Once I removed the weight of others' opinions from my shoulders, there was one lingering concern—my boys.

Would I be comfortable with my boys reading my book? If I was going to do this, we'd have to be okay with it because there was no way I would hide it. If I could be comfortable sharing my story with the world, I'd need to be comfortable sharing with my flesh and blood. Somehow, that felt even more scary. What would my sons think of their mom and her past antics? Would they be disappointed or embarrassed? Would word get around at school and cause teasing or bullying? (That's assuming anyone reads the book, which is a generous assumption, but still.) My boys were a big part of my reason for choosing to live an alcohol-free life, so I certainly didn't want to hurt them.

I spent lots of time agonizing over this and ultimately decided that the best gift I can give my children is to teach them the power of vulnerability and courage. I want to teach them it's okay to be open and honest with the world and that we can grow and learn from past mistakes. Those mistakes don't define us; they give us opportunities to improve. I have an open and honest relationship with them already, and although they aren't quite old enough to understand all these issues with alcohol, they soon will be. I'll need to have these conversations with them soon to prepare them for high school and college.

Around my eight-month "soberversary," we enjoyed spring break at the lake for a week of family time. One night we played a game called Kids Against Maturity, a family-friendly version of Cards Against Humanity. Think tons of potty humor. Tons. It always results in belly laughs and drinks being sprayed across the table. I had an answer card that read, "mom's purple red wine teeth." The card fit with one of the questions, so I played it, and I was curious to see what my youngest would say when he read it with the others to pick a winner. He immediately set it aside and said, "This one is stupid. It doesn't make sense because Mom doesn't even drink wine."

It was such a little moment, but it made me so happy inside. In my drinking days, I spent a lot of time with purple-red wine lips or teeth. I don't know if my kids ever noticed, but that the phrase was on a card in the game shows that many other kids *do* notice their moms' purple-red wine teeth. In this world of the "Mommy wine culture," it's a well-known phenomenon.

Now, my boys are an active part of my alcohol-free lifestyle. They know I quit drinking, they know why I quit drinking, and they know I've written a book and share about it on social media. We talk about it a lot, and I'm honest with them. They know their dad still drinks, and there's nothing wrong with that. We're showing them it's about honoring yourself and finding what works for you. I'm not naïve enough to think they'll never drink, but when they do someday, they'll understand alcohol from all angles.

My children gain nothing by me suppressing a big part of myself to protect them from the ugly parts of my past. They can learn from the mistakes I've made, and also from my choice to share them with the world. I want them to know that it's okay to make mistakes in your life and that those mistakes do not define you. I also want them to learn that you shouldn't be afraid to share your authentic self with those you love. My greatest hope is that they'll someday be proud of me for my choices, but whatever their reaction is, we'll get through it as a family.

14

The Rise and Fall of Badley

When I was little, my favorite uncle used to joke that I had a twin named BADLEY (not HADLEY—get it?), who was the real culprit whenever I did something wrong. She lived in the attic and only came out to cause trouble. I was a pretty good kid, so Badley wasn't very active.

Somehow in college, that nickname was resurrected and adapted to represent *drunk* Hadley. My friends laughed about my alter ego, Badley, and how hilarious she was. Everyone loved Badley and egged her on. Friends would constantly say things like, "Can Badley please come out tonight?" or "We haven't seen Badley in a while; we miss her!" Maybe it's because I am typically such a rule-following, type-A perfectionist, and people liked the fun, silly, and less responsible version of me. Maybe it's because, as a society, we celebrate and glorify drunkenness. Perhaps it's because we always secretly hope someone else at the party is drunker than we are.

Jokes about the Hadley/Badley dichotomy continued well into my adulthood. It was all good-natured joking, and I rolled my eyes and chuckled with everyone. Still, I had some pretty strong feelings about Badley and her antics.

I hated her with a passion. I always wondered if Badley was just a more extreme version of me, or was she totally different? Did she represent my true thoughts, feelings, and moral compass, or was she a loose cannon? After Badley came out to play, I would wake up the following day feeling suffocated by an emotion I hadn't yet identified as shame. Whatever it was, it weighed on my chest so heavily that I wanted to melt away into my sheets. I would eventually get up and do my typical morning checks. I looked at my phone for evidence of what happened and racked my brain, trying to remember the night. I looked for my purse, credit cards, and checked for bruises. Then, I would wallow in misery and tell myself I would never drink again. I would try to sleep away the day and avoid any mention of the night before.

I wanted to shrivel up and die whenever someone told a "funny" Badley story, like the one where I blacked out and slept outside the front door of the sorority house after bruising my fists from knocking for so long to have someone let me in. Or the time at a music festival when I lost a shoe while crowd surfing, took the metro home alone, and only remembered the tail end of the trip. Or the time I fell out of my loft senior year and broke my ribs, ending up in the emergency room with no recollection of what had happened. I could go on and on with examples of Badley's reckless, risky behavior. It was humiliating, humbling, and destructive. Nothing about it was amusing, yet it was celebrated and encouraged. I wasn't the only person these things were happening to, although I do not know if my friends felt the same level of self-loathing from their own blackout experiences.

Almost all the big, messy emotions I associate with my drinking habits stem from that tendency to black out. I always imagined the worst of myself from those moments of darkness. I pictured myself making out with a friend's boyfriend, starting a fight, or streaking naked across the Virginia Tech drill field. I was terrified, thinking someone out there had seen me at my worst and was privy to the humiliating things I had done. For weeks afterward, I was afraid to run into people I might have encountered during a blackout. I created crazy scenarios in my mind of things that might have happened, but I didn't want anyone to give me the actual details. I refused to let my best friend tell me what happened one particularly drunken night for *years* afterward. If I didn't know, I could feel a little more innocent. When I finally let her tell me, well into adulthood, I wished I hadn't and had continued on, blissfully unaware.

I used to pretend that I knew where the line was that kept me from getting to a point of no return, but there's no way to know. There were periods in my life when blackouts happened more frequently (college) and periods when they rarely happened (motherhood). It still happened, though, and even once a year is too often. Almost all those nights started the same way, with me swearing I'd be "good" and would only have a few drinks. They always ended with me waking up, realizing I had broken another promise to myself.

If you've never blacked out, you might not understand. It's not about hazy memories of the night before; it's about *zero* memories of the night before. It's terrifying, and I can't believe I let it continue for so long. My theory was that most people seemed to drink too much and would eventually puke. Not me. I've only thrown up from drinking twice in my life. Badge of honor, right? Instead, when I drank too much, my brain seemed to shut down and power off. No memories whatsoever. I had plenty of other friends who were also blackout drinkers, and it's not something anyone seemed to be ashamed of or worried about, although maybe they were dying on the inside like I was.

It seems like pure luck that nothing tragic or traumatic happened to me over the years. I can't even talk about spring break in Acapulco without thinking of all that could have gone wrong. I'll take some of those stories straight to my grave, knowing I'm lucky as hell to have survived. Several friends are probably sighing in relief as they realize I'm not going into the details of that one night at the club in Mexico …

I frequently spiral into a state of wonder and gratitude, thankful I survived my stupidity and went on to live a happy and productive life. Any of my blackout incidents easily could have had a very different ending. I sometimes have irrational fears that karma is waiting to circle back for me. I have felt the knot of shame closing around my heart even as I write because these memories (or lack thereof) are still so raw and tender to the touch. I have to remind myself I will never feel that way again. I will never black out and wake up shrouded in fear and uncertainty. I'll never close my eyes and desperately wish for a time machine to help me undo my choices from the night before. I'll never feel a hangover that lasts for a week and sends me spiraling into a depressive vortex. I'll never wonder if my husband or friends are mad at me and whether I deserve it. *Never again*.

On any day of the week, I can now wake up, look in the mirror, and say I love the person looking back at me. That would have been challenging to say on a post-blackout morning when I felt like a tattered shell of a person. Now, I'm a better mom, wife, friend, and human. I'm far from perfect, but I no longer suffer from these self-inflicted injuries.

Badley is dead to me—and good riddance!

15

The Shame Swamp

That first time I drank and got busted spectacularly, I felt intense shame over disappointing my parents and deviating from the core values I aligned with. Looking back, I can clearly see the shame cycle beginning with that first drinking experience. It continued as I drank my way through college and into my adult years. After each drinking or blackout episode, I would wake up crushed by a hangover, a sense of dread, and a fog of shame that threatened to drown me. I now refer to it as the Shame Swamp. It felt like that scene in *The Neverending Story* where Atreyu's horse gets sucked under the quicksand in the Swamp of Sadness. When I would wake up after drinking too much, I felt like Artax, the horse, slowly getting sucked under. These cumulative episodes led me to the conclusion that I was somehow flawed.

Each time I woke up, I would run through the same laundry list of questions as I beat myself up: What happened last night? Did I do anything stupid? Is anyone mad at me? What did I say and do? Where is my phone, my purse, my ID? Who saw me? What kind of person am I?

These thoughts played on a devastatingly consistent loop in my head the morning after drinking for my entire life. After every blackout, I was disgusted with myself and would swear never to let it happen again. News flash: it always did.

As I got older and entered adult life and parenthood, those episodes were few and far between, but they still happened. When they did, my time in the Shame Swamp was even more intense. It seemed to reinforce the notion that, *yes*, I was damaged goods. The stakes felt higher, so the shame was even heavier. What if I did something awful? What if my kids saw me? What if … what if … what if?

After a heavy drinking episode, the shame would be the most intense for the first few days. It would be all I thought about as I agonized over what might have happened and the things I might have done. Then, the shame would slowly fade away and become easier to bury with time. If I learned I hadn't done anything crazy or inappropriate or that everyone else had been as drunk as I was (halleluiah), it would speed up my shame recovery.

After a blackout, the resulting shame spiral often would lead me to give up drinking for a while. It might scare me straight for a week, a few weeks, or even a month. Eventually, I'd soften on my "I'm never drinking again" stance and ease my way back in, ultimately ending up right back where I started. It seems absurd that this happened over and over for more than twenty-five years without me being able to identify the emotion I was feeling. It's easy to look back now and recognize it as shame, but for a long time, I didn't have a word for what I was feeling.

I've read much of the incredible Brené Brown's work and especially love her research and anecdotes on shame. I always found it incredibly interesting, but I never really thought it applied to me. What on earth did I have to feel ashamed of? I was a successful woman with a beautiful family and a solid life. Picture perfect, remember? I was still drawn to her work and devoured her books and podcasts without really understanding why I connected to them so much.

Finally, within the last few years, I had a wake-up call of epic proportions. It was like Brené smacked me in the face and told me to open my eyes. Finally, I could see that the emotion I'd been feeling and suppressing for *so* long was, in fact, shame. Dark, dirty, secretive, and suffocating. That's how it always felt in my chest, like something with a slimy hand was gripping my heart and wouldn't let go. I never identified the feeling, and I never confronted it. I let it simmer for years until I slowly recognized it.

There are lots of definitions of shame out there, but the one that resonates with me the most is straight from Brené. She says, "Shame is an intensely painful feeling or experience of believing that we are flawed and therefore unworthy of love, belonging, and connection."[1]

A lot of my shame stemmed from the idea that I seemed to live my life as two separate people, and I couldn't reconcile the differences. There was Hadley, who was responsible, mature, classy, hardworking, and considered herself to be incredibly ethical with a firm moral compass. Hadley was Type A and introverted. She was a planner, and she had a killer work ethic. She was the friend who held on to everyone's passports and money when we went on spring break. Hadley was a leader and a stereotypical only-child overachiever.

Then Hadley would drink too much, and Badley would come out to play. Badley was loud, sloppy, and belligerent. Badley was the *all* to Hadley's *nothing*. She made questionable decisions and was irresponsible and obnoxious. She spent too much money, couldn't keep track of her purse, and always seemed to piss off her husband.

A profound, burning question haunted me. Was Badley a different person? Did she act in ways that were completely independent of Hadley? Was she off the rails and not to be trusted? Could she do things that were totally out of line with what Hadley would do? *Or* was Badley just a slightly louder and slurrier version of Hadley? Could she still be trusted to act in alignment with Hadley's moral compass? Could Badley still distinguish between right and wrong and act accordingly, or was she a free agent? I hoped it was the former, but I couldn't be sure.

This haunted me on those mornings after a blackout. I didn't know the answer, so I assumed the worst of myself when I couldn't remember the night. Maybe I robbed a bank or made out with Chris Hemsworth in front of my husband. Maybe I flashed my boobs to a school bus full of kids or smashed up an ATM. None of those things ever happened (to my knowledge), but damn, it was a scary feeling to wake up and assume you're a terrible person.

I never talked about any of this with anyone. Shame loves to live in the dark, where it grows like mold. Every time I drank, whether or not I blacked out, I'd add a little more shame to the collection. I let this build up inside me for decades like toxic sludge. Around the time of the infamous '80s birthday party, I started to identify and become more aware of what I was feeling. It felt like something I might fix, and that sounded magical.

Shame feels dirty and private, so our first instinct is to bury it deep and keep it hidden. That's what I did for so long, and it took a toll on my psyche. Then I realized I was giving it more power to hurt me by keeping it inside. Once I talked about how I felt, shared my experience, and acknowledged how drinking led to these intense feelings of shame, I broke free from it all.

Shame is like a vampire that shrivels up when the sun shines on it. It loses its power and turns to dust. So, my goal has been to open up and talk about that shame as much as possible until none of it is left. And with my drinking days behind me, I know I won't be adding any new shame to the collection. It's a beautiful feeling.

16

Learning from Regret

Besides the shame I felt from my drinking, there was an almost constant sense of regret from so many of my supposedly fabulous and "fun" party-girl experiences. Shame and regret are two emotions that are intimately connected.

One Halloween, less than two weeks before my first marathon, our neighbors threw a party. Even though I'd been meticulously training for this race, I decided it was a great time to throw down and get hammered. I'm sure I went into the night, as usual, claiming that I would only have a few drinks. The next thing I knew, we were all swinging from the proverbial chandeliers and passing around a breathalyzer test as a joke. This was a poor choice on so many levels. Not only did the breathalyzer confirm that I was incredibly intoxicated, but sharing it with everyone at the party guaranteed that I'd wake up a few days later with one of the worst colds of my life. Not a great choice before running a 26.2-mile race you've been preparing for over six long, grueling months.

There were so many things to regret about this scenario, and I spent the next ten days before my race mentally working through each of them in agonizing detail. Years later, I still cringe when I think about that night. First, I know I drank too much and drank it way too quickly, as was my M.O. I've never been able to sip a drink, whether we're talking about water, celery juice, *or* the mystery Halloween punch. If there's a drink in my hand, I'll chug it in seconds. I firmly believe this is why I was always prone to blacking out, as rapid rises in blood alcohol content seem to be associated with the phenomenon.

Next, why did a bunch of grown-ass adults think it was amusing to blow into a breathalyzer? Why did we think it was funny to see how high each of us could register, like some twisted competition to get the closest to alcohol poisoning without landing in the hospital? I'll never know, and unfortunately, I can't go back in time to figure it out.

Lastly, why did my normally germophobic self think it was appropriate to put my mouth on something being passed around a party like a bong in prime cold and flu season? Under normal circumstances, even pre-COVID, that thought is enough to make me barf in my mouth. It's just what happened when Badley took control.

The week before my race, I should have been resting, fueling, and mentally preparing myself for the biggest physical challenge I had ever attempted. Instead, I was dealing with a hangover from hell and a cough that was getting worse by the day. I was so mad at myself. I felt like I'd thrown away hours and miles of hard work to get ready for this race. It was the most intense sense of regret I had ever experienced. I spent a lot of time beating myself up over this self-inflected nightmare. I coughed and hacked even as I pulled up to the hotel the night before the race, praying my lungs would hold out and allow me to get through it. They did, and I still managed to run a pretty phenomenal race, but I'll always wonder how I would have performed that day if I'd gone into it differently. If I'd been healthy, rested, and prepared instead of sick as a dog and barely recovered from one of the worst hangovers of my life.

On paper, regret is the emotion of wishing one had made a different decision in the past because the consequences of the decision were unfavorable. In *Atlas of the Heart*, Brené Brown clarifies that with regret, "We believe the outcome was caused by our decisions or actions."[1]

Regret is *I did something bad*, while shame is *I AM bad*. It seems only natural that living in a constant state of regret, thinking *I did something bad*, will ultimately lead to the faulty conclusion, "I am bad."

In real life, regret is that angsty feeling gripping your heart and brain as you replay an event or scenario over and over in your mind, wishing you could hit a magical re-do button. It's that sinking sensation you experience when you desperately wish you could fix or change something you did in the past, but you know it's not possible. When you walk through all the scenarios *other* than the one that ultimately played out, wishing you could go back in time and make a different choice.

While I constantly experienced that kind of regret with my drinking, I can honestly say I don't hold on to regrets for many other things in life. I'm talking about the good, honest mistakes and mishaps we all make. I made a point to learn from them and grow from them all. I didn't dwell on them, and as a result, they shaped me and molded me into the person I am.

I truly get the "no regrets" philosophy, but honestly, I don't believe regrets are bad if we use them as a learning opportunity and then release them appropriately. In retrospect, I'm glad I regret so many of the times when I drank. I sometimes wish I could go back and hit the re-do button, but those regrets (and there were many) ultimately led me to decide I'd had enough.

Those regrets led me to decide that alcohol didn't have a place in my life anymore. Those regrets were my mind's way of telling me I was veering off track at a rapid pace. Those regrets made me decide I wanted to do better and be better.

I'm still working to forgive myself and let go of my regret over things that happened when I was drinking. I tell myself that's not who I am anymore; I've grown and evolved, and there's no use wasting mental energy on rehashing the past. I try to be grateful for those regrets because their cumulative impact led to one of the best decisions of my life and one thing I'll never regret—choosing to live an alcohol-free life. My past mistakes do not define me. I get the chance to be better because of them.

Forgiving ourselves is more art than science. It takes work and time, and it's not always linear. You can start by thinking of all the things you know you need to forgive yourself for and the regrets you need to let go of. Say them out loud. Accept them and take responsibility for them. Think about how they're making you feel *and* how they're holding you back. Now, show yourself some compassion. Think of how you would respond to a friend if they came to you with a list of their regrets. You'd respond with kindness and assure them they were worthy of forgiveness. Now, respond to your inner critic with that same kind voice.

If you find yourself hung up on your regrets and struggling to forgive yourself, it's time to let go of the past and turn your focus toward the future. Here are some ideas to help you look forward with hope and optimism to leave the regrets behind:

Remind yourself that you're choosing to release your regrets and move on. The past is the past, and it's a waste of time to dwell on it.

Think about what lesson your regrets have taught you. Cull out the positives. What can you learn from them before you tuck them away?

Tell yourself that your drunk behavior was just that, drunk behavior. It's no indication of any deeper character flaws, and it's not full of some mysterious deeper meaning.

Remind yourself that while you may have some bridges to mend, no one else is dwelling on your drunken regrets.

Focus on the future and work to make memories you feel good about. Celebrate them as they happen and let them crowd out the memories of those drunken regrets.

I don't believe that regrets are inherently bad, and the goal isn't to avoid them completely, but we don't want to live a life riddled with them, keeping us stuck in a pattern of negativity. When we face those inevitable regrets, let's view them as an opportunity to learn, make amends, and be brave. That's certainly what I tried to do. Choosing sobriety as an answer to regret felt like one of the bravest things I had ever done.

17

Kicking Mommy Wine Culture to the Curb

Wine and parenting: at what point in the last few decades did we come to associate the two? When did we decide that a giant glass of pinot should symbolize women's liberation and badassery? How did it become the salve for soothing the wounds of the Mommy Wars? It's as though *big alcohol* conspired with pop culture to make women believe that wine was the key to finding that elusive concept of balance. "Want to have it all as a modern mother? With wine, you can!"

I struggled with how to talk about the mommy wine culture because, honestly, it makes me feel like a big, fat fraud. For years, I bought into the hype. When I first launched myself on social media, I leaned into it heavily. I used my platform to perpetuate the idea that drinking wine was cool, normal, and the key to surviving mommyhood. I refuse to delete all the stupid things I've posted in the past because it's like a roadmap of my growth. You can scroll back through my Instagram account and see my stupidity in all its glory.

I proudly posted pictures of the coffee mug my stepson gave me that said, "This Might Be Wine." I promoted "wine workouts" each Friday that included a bottle or glass of wine. I did hilarious (insert eye roll emoji) posts about desperately needing wine after a long day or week with my kids. I talked about how much wine we needed to stock up on when a big snowstorm came and shared all the little cartoons about wine and coffee fighting over who I loved the most. When the pandemic hit, you bet I was cracking all kinds of "it's five o'clock somewhere" jokes.

It turns out that jokes on the internet aren't just jokes on the internet. Even if our kids don't see the boozy memes on Facebook, these trends perpetuate the notion that alcohol is the answer to every problem. Social media, along with all the other sources that sell this story, have woven a powerful narrative about the role that alcohol should play in our lives. We're naïve if we think that doesn't have a direct impact on how we move through the world. We regularly buy things from ads and influencers on Facebook and Instagram. Social media convinces us we *need* the newest magical shampoo or exercise device or that shirt our favorite blogger has on. It's no surprise we're also buying the subliminal messages about the role booze should play in our lives.

I wasn't leading the charge on any of this wine-fueled internet banter. I was a follower. I was trying to fit in with my perceived niche: moms of young kids who love wine but want to be healthy. Gag me. There's a whole industry devoted to this niche. We buy wine glasses that sport slogans like "Mommy's sippy cup" or shirts that say, "Working Nine to WINE." We plan playdates for our kids around the moms who will booze it up with us while the kids play with Legos. We buy bottles with pink labels called "Yes Way Rosé." Our kids come home from preschool with artwork showing mommy with her nightly glass of wine, and we share it on Facebook with pride. The message is clear to everyone, including our kids: Being a parent is challenging and exhausting. The only way to survive and be happy is to drink alcohol to numb ourselves.

Sorry kiddo, I can only tolerate you if I first drink some of this wine. Otherwise, you're unbearable.

We encourage these connections daily:

My kid threw a tantrum—drink wine.

School was canceled—drink wine.

I chaperoned a field trip today—drink wine.

My kid is practicing his recorder—drink wine.

Kids are home sick with the flu—drink wine.

It appears to be the perfect, one-size-fits-all solution! What the hell have we done to ourselves? When we have babies, we're expected to bounce back immediately. We are burdened with unrealistic expectations about how our bodies should look and respond after giving birth. As moms, we often endure most of the mental and physical load of child-rearing. It can be stressful and isolating. We don't need wine; we need more help. We need better health care, better maternity leave policies, better mental health resources, equal pay, and high-quality childcare. We need to focus on *really* taking care of ourselves. The mommy wine culture teaches us that drinking solves our parenting struggles when, in reality, it's making things worse. It's giving us more problems, not less; it's chipping away at our mental health, and it's distracting us from the things that could genuinely provide relief and support.

Another reason the mommy-wine connection is so toxic is that, to put it bluntly, it's setting a horrible example for our kids. Trust me, they're paying attention. It was all fun and games while my kids were too young to know what was happening. They saw me drinking wine, and I'm sure some of this seeped into their subconscious, but they didn't get the nuances of alcohol. They didn't know what it meant to be drunk or what a hangover was.

As they started getting a little older, it became clear they were noticing more. They picked up on things in TV shows or movies and understood what it meant when someone was drunk. They watched us mix fun drinks at the lake and saw forty amazing friends each deliver a bottle of wine to our door on my fortieth birthday during the pandemic. They saw me pour a big glass of wine while I watched the news each evening. Drinking was a big part of my life, and I was feeling more uncomfortable with that as time went on, and I saw it through my children's eyes.

My boys were a huge part of my wake-up call the summer I quit drinking. I noticed these patterns and realized it was not the example I wanted to set for them. They were at the age where they were like sponges, soaking up everything around them and saving it for later use, especially anything related to the grown-up world. It hit me that everything they were seeing and hearing would have a direct impact on how they viewed alcohol and drinking in their teenage years, which were right around the corner. I was suddenly terrified when I realized I was sending them lots of messages about drinking that they would save and hold on to. Messages like: When you're an adult, you drink when you're stressed out or overwhelmed. Drinking is how you have fun. Drinking is how you cope when your life is complicated and parenting is tough.

I lost sleep many nights thinking about how I did *not* want them to repeat my mistakes in high school and college. I didn't want them to hit forty before they realized getting shit-faced regularly wasn't normal or healthy. I certainly didn't want them to think that being their parent made me need to drink.

As my younger kids rapidly approach their teen years, I'm terrified of what's to come. I hear startling stories coming from my cushy, suburban oasis about parents letting their high schoolers and their friends drink at home. Some appear to be purchasing booze for the kids, and others just give them a place to drink it. They think they're providing a safe and controlled environment for the inevitable. They assume the kids are going to do it anyway, so they might as well allow it. Or maybe they just want to be the cool parents, caring more about being besties with their teens than actual parents. I frequently hear the flawed theory that allowing kids to drink a little with you at home teaches them to respect alcohol and not make it such a taboo thing.

The problem with all of this, frankly, is that it's bullshit. There is *zero* evidence supporting those theories. In fact, the data shows the opposite to be true. One of the most significant risk factors for developing Alcohol Use Disorder is drinking at an early age. The earlier you drink, the more likely you are to develop a problem at some point in life. One study from the National Institute on Alcohol Abuse and Alcoholism showed that of those individuals who began drinking before age fourteen, 47 percent experienced dependence at some point.[1] It also showed that for each year earlier than twenty-one that someone drank, the greater the odds that they would develop a problem. They go on to say, "If parents provide alcohol to their kids (even small amounts), have positive attitudes about drinking, and engage in alcohol misuse, adolescents have an increased risk of misusing alcohol."

These parents aren't doing their kids any favors by allowing them to chug White Claw in the basement, regardless of how they try to rationalize it. I hope they have some killer umbrella insurance policies, too, because I can't imagine taking on the liability associated with those decisions.

Parents of our generation have a more demanding job than any before us. Gone are the days of sending your kids out to play until dark without knowing where they are or what they're doing. We have so much to worry about that it's hard to choose where to focus our parental energy. Technology, screen time, school shootings, bullying, sports, and whether our kids need to take college-level courses in preschool. Parenting has become intense and competitive. We have to be on our A-game, or else we're convinced our kids won't thrive in this crazy world we now live in. Throw in a pandemic, racial tensions, fights over Critical Race Theory and gun control, and we could live in a constant state of parental anxiety.

And there isn't much support for parents, especially mothers. No matter how much progress we've made, the popular quote still applies: "We're expected to work like we aren't mothers and mother like we don't work." The pandemic highlighted this dramatically as we bore the brunt of the burden—working from home while overseeing our children's virtual schooling or trying to tackle homeschooling. We were expected to function normally without childcare, and many women gave up or lost their jobs. We made impossible decisions daily. It's no wonder that women's drinking escalated dramatically during COVID.

Mommy Wine Culture has taught us that alcohol is the answer to just about every problem. I have no doubt that Big Alcohol has been behind the scenes pulling the levers on this racket. They have capitalized on the lack of societal support for mothers and helped push us down this path where we recognize booze as the best way to lighten our load and decompress from it all. They've made entire generations of women believe that drinking signifies independence in the modern mother.

Instead of further liberating us, as they try to sell it, it's harming us. It's normalizing the notion that we need a carcinogenic drug putting us in an altered state to make motherhood tolerable. How are we supposed to teach our children appropriate problem-solving skills or equip them with the tools to manage stress and tough decisions if we think wine is the answer? If we perpetuate this cycle, we play right into Big Alcohol's hands. We're right where they want us.

Unplugging from the mommy-wine matrix is essential. Even if you aren't interested in eliminating alcohol altogether, you can still play a significant role in breaking the connection between booze and parenting, ultimately doing women everywhere a huge favor. This is an issue that impacts all of us as mothers. It's a feminist issue, really, so by closing the door on the mommy-wine agenda, we're elevating *all* women.

How do we unplug from it all? The first thing we can do is *stop* buying into it. Stop giving our money to products and people that encourage the connection between motherhood and alcohol. When I stopped drinking, I cleaned house, finding all the cups with mommy wine slogans, workout tanks, seltzer cozies, an apron, dish towels, and even some wine artwork. It all glorified drinking, and it felt great to trash it.

What products do you have that support or encourage the mommy-wine connection? Ask yourself this: what message do they send your kids, and what message do they send to the world? Do you want your kids to look at a dish towel each day that says, "Boxed wine is just a juice box for moms?"

Then, consider how you talk about drinking, online and in real life. Do you regularly post or share memes about drinking and how much you need your wine because the kids are home sick or because little Johnny needs help with his long division? I ask this without judgment because I used to be horrible at this. I built my whole online persona around how much I loved and needed wine.

Can we take a stand here, too? Stop and think before you post, share, or even like a post encouraging drinking. The more we refuse to take part, the more progress we'll make. I did a complete 180, eliminating alcohol as a subject and taking a stand in the opposite direction. You have the right to change your opinions as you learn and grow.

Next, consider how you talk about alcohol at home and what messages it might send your kids. Do you say things like I used to say, proclaiming loudly that you need a drink because it was a long day? Do you dramatically pour a glass of wine during a painful homework session? How do you talk about drinking with other women? Can you avoid getting sucked into mommy-wine banter?

The goal is to become more aware of how you participate in the mommy-wine phenomenon and look for ways to unplug—to refuse to associate with something that negatively impacts mothers and children.

The intent behind my sobriety certainly wasn't to give a big FU to the patriarchy, but I see it as an unexpected bonus. The radical choice to be alcohol-free in a world desperately trying to get more women drinking, feels like a great way to stick it to The Man. As women, we are still fighting for our freedom and equality, and we can't do that effectively if we're all comfortably numb and buzzed from our "mommy juice."

18

The Joys of Sober Parenting

When my son, Caden, was born, I knew immediately what kind of mother I wanted to be. I envisioned myself with the patience of Mother Teresa as I made homemade baby food and did educational crafts with my children all day. We would sing songs and hold hands, and they'd be little angels who could read by the age of three. I was going to *crush* motherhood.

You can probably guess how that turned out. I soon realized that I was indeed a great mom, but none of those expectations panned out. Sometimes, we did crafts, and sometimes, we sang songs, and sometimes, my kids threw temper tantrums and bit me as I tried to buckle them in their car seats. I loved them so much I wanted to explode one minute, and the next, I was screaming into a pillow and crying for twenty-four hours straight.

As much as I loved being a mom, it provided countless opportunities to drink away the crazies while I still believed alcohol was the answer. Stress, worry, tough decisions, exhaustion, anger, frustration, and more exhaustion. It comes with the territory. Then, layer on the logistical aspect of motherhood: sports schedules, school projects, PTA meetings, doctor appointments, field trip forms, and dress-up days at school. It's easy to focus on the frustrations and get sucked into a negative mindset. Kids won't adjust to the time change? *Ugh*, I need a drink. Someone had a bad report card? Open a bottle! Crazy week of practices and activities? Chug-a-lug!

As I neared the end of my drinking days, I paid more attention to the impact booze had on my time and relationship with my kids, and I noticed a distinct trend. When I was stressed, worn out, or upset, I poured myself a big glass of wine to deal with it. Then, I retreated into myself and ignored my family. It didn't make me relaxed and carefree; it made me cranky and short-tempered. I would focus all my energy on the negatives and fixate on how stressed and miserable I was. I would go to bed with a headache, wake up after getting poor-quality sleep, and start the process all over again. I always felt restless, like I wasn't actually enjoying my time with my family or absorbing all the joy that should go along with being a mom. I was dwelling on the booze I thought was necessary to make it more tolerable. Nothing about drinking made parenting any easier. In fact, it had the opposite effect. Drinking was making motherhood unpleasant.

I didn't have this figured out when I first decided to eliminate alcohol, but I noticed an interesting change soon after. When I stopped turning to my glass of wine each evening, I discovered I felt more positive about my day and was much more patient with my kids. I found myself enjoying the evening hours with my family and being more connected and present with what was happening in the house. I started noticing all the happy, joyful moments instead of fixating on the negative ones. I wasn't in a foul mood every evening. For the first time in a long time, I didn't feel like I had to hide from the challenges of motherhood. I was much more prepared to tackle them head-on, and I found them much less stressful than I had in the past.

I started taking self-care more seriously, realizing it wasn't just about getting a manicure or taking a bubble bath. Self-care became a daily practice. I looked inward to determine what I needed on a deeper level. Did I need more alone time, more sleep, more support from my husband, more time with friends? Did I need to give myself more grace, or even find a therapist? When I paid attention to what I really needed and stopped Band-Aiding over motherhood with wine, life felt easier. I was more confident as a mom when I wasn't cowering behind a buzz to make things feel more manageable. Sobriety was the first thing I had tried that actually made parenting feel easier. Who would have thought?

It seemed counter-intuitive after spending so many years believing a nice glass of red was the only way to unwind after a long day. I was shocked to realize that wine had been acting as a buffer that kept me from enjoying big chunks of my life. Yes, parenting is tough, and being a mom still presents constant challenges. I finally understand the saying, "little kids, little problems—big kids, big problems." Now, I have one teenager and one pre-teen, and there is so much to worry about as they get older. I'm much more prepared to handle it now. I'm ready. I know that a drink will solve nothing, and it will not make parenting easier.

You might think, "Okay, I get what's wrong with Mommy Wine Culture in theory, but how the hell am I actually supposed to survive as a mom without alcohol?" The thought seemed daunting when I first considered a sober lifestyle. I had been so conditioned to think of my wine as "mommy's little helper" that I convinced myself it was a necessary part of surviving parenthood. Turns out, it wasn't essential at all. It was more like a weight, pulling me down as I tried to tread water and keep my head above the surface. My goal isn't just to crap all over Mommy Wine

Culture. It's to offer proof and hope that parenting is actually a hundred times more fulfilling and enjoyable when booze is out of the picture.

As moms, we expect to face constant challenges. We learn to expect the unexpected. Motherhood is a wild ride, and we have to hold on as best we can through all the turns, dips, and peaks. And just like on a roller-coaster, sometimes we want to barf, sometimes we want to scream, and sometimes we want to throw our hands up in joy.

When we rely on alcohol to solve these problems and make parenting "easier," it does several things. Because it keeps us focused on the relief we think we're getting from the drink, we don't do things that will fill our metaphorical cups and truly make us feel better and more equipped to handle parenting. Drinking is not self-care. When we look to booze for the answers to our problems, we're not, for example, getting extra quality sleep and carving out time to read a book or meditate. We're instead chugging wine while bitching about our little monsters and then going to bed late with a headache. We aren't problem-solving and thinking rationally about how to address issues that arise. We procrastinate on implementing solutions and try to soothe ourselves superficially. It also conditions us to see the negatives more than the positives, as we're constantly tallying the reasons we're going to deserve that drink at five o'clock. Using booze to self-medicate our way through motherhood might make us more laid back and relaxed at first, but it ultimately adds to our anxiety and has a negative impact on our overall mental health. Finally, drinking to cope with parenting challenges distances us from our kids and makes us more detached and less present. We pay less attention, care a little less, and lean away when we should lean in.

I set a good example for my boys now, which further bolsters my confidence as a mother and makes me increasingly proud of this decision. They see drinking and drunkenness depicted in movies, TV, social media, and, from time to time, in real life with our friends. They understand it's a choice they'll have to make someday. They see me navigating sobriety with a newfound passion for life, and I'm demonstrating that it isn't boring, unpleasant, or uncool. I'm showing that the old standard of binge drinking through your youth isn't the *only* path, as I once believed as a teenager.

I always said that when my kids are teenagers, I'll tell them they can call me with no questions asked, and I'll come to get them if they're in a bad situation. The chances were slim while I was still drinking that I'd be able to drive if they called me on a Saturday night. That realization hit me hard. What if my son needed a sober ride, and I couldn't provide one? It gives me so much peace to know that isn't an issue anymore. They can count on me to be their getaway car. They can count on me in simple daily situations also, just knowing that what they see is what they get. I'm not vacillating between buzzed mom and sober mom, with wildly different moods and tolerance levels between the two. There's only one version of me, and she is mature, responsible, and ready for whatever curveballs this crazy bunch of boys is sure to send my way in the next few years.

Changing my relationship with alcohol allowed me to rediscover the joy of being a mom and powerfully reconnect with my kids. My mindset is so much more positive, and I'm thrilled that I'll get to fully enjoy my time with them over the next few years. I'm still no Mother Teresa, but I'm exponentially more patient than I was when I was drinking. My nerves are no longer frayed and raw, and I handle my frustrations with more grace and dignity.

This is what we're missing out on when we give in to the demands of the Mommy Wine Culture. We're unknowingly draining the joy out of motherhood and numbing ourselves. It's a tremendous loss, and we don't even realize it's happening until it's too late.

19

Booze & Marriage

The question I get asked most frequently since sharing my journey publicly is whether my husband still drinks and, if so, how I handle that. Unpacking the role that alcohol plays in our relationships can be a complicated issue. It was one that I worried about at first, given the significant role alcohol had played in our marriage over the years.

My husband does still drink, but as I've mentioned, he is a miraculous "moderation unicorn." His relationship with alcohol is very different than mine. He can take it or leave it. He rarely over-indulges and has probably never felt ashamed of his drinking.

I didn't expect or ask him to quit alongside me. I know, in my heart, that if I had needed him to in order for me to be successful, he would have done it. If my problem had been of a different severity, and I couldn't take him having an occasional drink in front of me, I feel confident that he would have been willing to quit in order to help me.

When I first decided to quit drinking, my husband was genuinely confused and surprised. He didn't know that I was struggling. I had kept all my issues stuffed deep down inside for so long, and I was great at acting like everything was fine. There were no glaring red flags or outward consequences.

He was immediately supportive, but I don't think he believed it would stick. He assumed it was just a phase, like all those times during an epic hangover when I announced, "I'm never drinking again!"

So, now that we're a few years down the road and it clearly *stuck*, how do I handle his drinking, and does it bother me?

Let's be honest—it depends on my mood. 97% of the time, I genuinely don't care.

I realized early on that, like so many other parts of marriage, communication is key. I had to open up and talk to him about what I was doing and feeling, ask for his support, and create some boundaries. For me, those initial boundaries were things like:

I don't care if you drink bourbon or beer, but please don't open a bottle of red wine at home. That felt like a big trigger for me.

Don't leave your glass in the sink for me to smell or wash.

I don't want to have to buy alcohol, so you have to keep yourself stocked.

Over time, those boundaries have evolved a bit, and I think that's normal and natural. I would now add a few things like:

I won't do all the driving around with the kids in the evenings because you want to have a drink.

Let's plan a date night sometimes where there is no drinking so we're on the same page.

I still don't want to buy it, but if you need a case of beer from Costco and I'm there, I'm not going to make you take a separate trip for it.

Another important boundary for me is being mindful of how it's discussed and portrayed in front of our boys. We talk about "mommy-wine culture," but honestly, dads fall into the same trap. If you're going to have a drink, just do it. Don't make it a big production with "Damn, I need a drink!" or "Come to Poppa" kind of vibes. That behavior gives me the ICK. It's a drink (well, poison, actually), not a magical elixir or problem solver. Let's not glamorize or romanticize it any more than popular culture already does.

You might need more aggressive boundaries than mine, at least in the beginning. Don't feel bad about that. Your relationship should be a safe space to practice advocating for yourself. That's a handy skill to have in sobriety. Maybe you don't think you can deal with having any alcohol in the home. Maybe you don't want to be around if they're drinking. Maybe you need a break from all social events until you feel more confident. You have to share your concerns with your partner and be very clear about what you need.

I said that his drinking doesn't bother me 97% of the time, and that's true, I think, because he rarely overindulges. On the rare occasions that he does, I have no problem telling him that it's annoying. If you've ever been one-on-one with someone who is drunk while you're sober, it's irritating. That's no secret. It's hard to connect and have a meaningful conversation when someone is intoxicated. That doesn't mean I forbid him from ever getting drunk; it just means that it's not my favorite way to hang out. If I'm being honest, it's also pretty tough to be understanding of hangovers once you've chosen sobriety. I try, I swear.

Again, the key to all of this is communication. Like it or not, that's the key to most issues in marriage or relationships of any kind. I'm fortunate, I know, because my husband is supportive, and his drinking is not an issue for either of us. That's not the case for many people that I hear from in the sober-verse. Many of the people who ask me this question seem to be dealing with partners who are either unsupportive, very heavy drinkers themselves, or a combination of the two.

If your partner is also a problematic drinker, it might be hard for them to accept your choice because it's holding a mirror up to their own problem. We know that being ready is the first step to making a change with our drinking, and if they aren't ready, your decision might feel like a judgment against them. It might make them uncomfortable to see you ready for a change that they're not yet prepared to make. If that is the case, all you can do is talk to them, explain what you're doing, and ask for their support. You can't force them to be ready, but you have every right to ask for their support as you do what you need to do.

Maybe your partner doesn't have a problem, but they still seem generally unsupportive. Maybe they, like so many people, associate sobriety with boredom and think you'll no longer have fun together. Maybe drinking is a big part of your social life, and a change makes them nervous. There are so many myths and fallacies out there about alcohol. It's not surprising to see them pop up as couples begin exploring their relationship with alcohol.

Whatever the reason for their lack of support, you have to remember that your choice not to drink is an important one. You're entitled to it, and it's something you've chosen to improve your health and quality of life. It's not a choice you should have to compromise on for someone else's comfort.

At the end of the day, we have to do what's right for us. We can't keep drinking simply because our partner thinks we should or isn't showing adequate support. That's no way to go through life, and it's not something you should have to compromise on. You can't necessarily expect your partner to embrace sobriety for themselves, but you should be able to expect them to support your choice. If communication isn't going to cut it and they still refuse to be supportive, then maybe there are bigger problems to deal with, and therapy or a counselor is a good option to explore.

I know my own views and opinions on alcohol have changed so drastically that I sometimes sense my husband rolling his eyes on the inside. I can't help it; I've read, researched, and learned so much about alcohol and the damage it does that there's no going back for me. Although I try not to get preachy, my views are kind of extreme. It's an example of how we can change and evolve over time. That's a normal and beautiful part of life. When we're in a relationship, we have to be willing to love and accept our spouse/partner through those changes and evolutions. That's not always easy and sometimes comes with some trial and error.

I don't have a magical solution. I can only share what has worked for me. Communication, boundaries, empathy, and finding some common ground. Get help if you need it; find someone to talk to who can help you work through your issues. At the end of the day, quitting alcohol is going to help you become the best version of yourself, and that's one of the best possible things you can do for your relationship.

20

Letting Go of Fitting In

For much of my life, I felt like I didn't quite fit in. I was always on the edge of the popular crowd. I had to work hard to make those friendships happen; they never came easily, and they never felt natural. I was like a chameleon, changing myself to fit each situation. As a result, my relationships never felt nurturing and fulfilling. They felt empty. I knew if I stopped doing the "work" to fit in, I would slowly drift away, and no one would miss me. I wasn't a critical part of any group; I was just skirting around the outside looking in. I experienced deep insecurity in my social life.

Alcohol became my introvert armor. It made me feel more confident and outgoing than I was. It made it easier for me to play the role I thought others would like. Drinking felt essential to keeping up with this whole charade. Being the fun party girl would make me more likely to be remembered and included, and it also lessened the pain of feeling disposable.

In adulthood, I was lucky to make some phenomenal friends. I realized my worth and discovered that I wouldn't feel that insecurity when I was with the right people. I would never have to fight for my seat at the table. My seat would always be open with these women who loved, supported, and believed in one another. It taught me what friendship was supposed to look like, and it was beautiful.

This was a massive shift for me, and although it was a positive one, it took time to get used to. Alcohol was already embedded deep in my routines and psyche. It was the most used tool in my toolbox. I seemed to become increasingly introverted as I aged, so alcohol felt necessary for engaging in anything resembling small talk or for pushing through those moments when I'd rather be home with a book. Plus, it was everywhere. I certainly wasn't the only one drinking. It seemed like we were all ramping up the frequency and quantity.

When I knew I needed to eliminate alcohol, I worried it would be a death sentence for my social life. Would sobriety take away the sense of inclusion I finally felt after a lifetime of living on the fringe? I was terrified to do anything that went against the grain because experience taught me that was dangerous. I imagined myself wasting away at home with nothing to do. It was painful to imagine walking into a room and making small talk with my inhibitions left intact—heavy, clunky, and awkward.

It's interesting that alcohol is the only substance you need an explanation for quitting. No one would say, "OHHHH, you quit smoking? *Why?*" Or "You're never going to do cocaine again? What about special occasions?" With alcohol, you're supposed to be armed with an acceptable explanation, and even then, you know people will likely pick it apart.

Don't get me wrong; I don't *care* what people think or whether they try to pick apart my reasoning. I know it's probably a reflection of their own issues, blah blah blah. I was concerned I would constantly have to explain and worry that people would feel uncomfortable or act differently around me. But it hasn't been much of an issue. There have been a few bumps in the road, but for the most part, my close friends and family have met my decision with respect and kindness. I quit drinking because of the toll it was taking on my physical and mental health, and I feel one hundred times healthier and happier since quitting. The people firmly in my corner are thrilled to see me thriving. They get that my decision was about *me* and not about them. I have zero judgment for my friends who still drink. I'm not on some kind of anti-alcohol crusade. I simply did what was best for me.

I still receive my fair share of silly questions from acquaintances and strangers who can't grasp the concept of voluntarily eliminating alcohol. As a result, I've learned that "no thanks" and "I just don't drink" are complete sentences, and I don't owe anyone any kind of explanation.

My next concern was whether I could still have fun without alcohol in my life. I was afraid this decision might once again leave me feeling like an outsider, struggling to fit in.

Here's the thing about rebuilding an alcohol-free social life—it's not automatic. It takes some time for our fun sensors (let's pretend that's a scientific term) to re-calibrate when we remove alcohol from the equation. When we only experience fun through the lens of alcohol, we have to redefine what "fun" means. We have to get used to being fully present in every situation, not dulled and muted by a buzz. We must condition ourselves to no longer think that drinking makes something fun. As I figured this out for myself, it felt like putting glasses on for the first time and realizing how blurry my vision had gotten.

It takes patience and a deliberate mindset shift to accomplish this. If you are constantly equating drinking with fun, you're naturally going to think that any scenario without drinking will not be fun. Try to catch these thought patterns as they happen. Contrary to popular belief, it's not the booze that makes the concert, dinner, or party fun. It's being with your friends, getting out, dressing up, laughing, and enjoying good food. You decide if you're going to have fun or not—fun isn't something that just happens to you. Don't assume it won't be fun because you aren't drinking. Instead, decide it *will* be fun because you aren't drinking. Then, think about how amazing you'll feel the next day.

I have so much more fun doing *everything* now because I'm experiencing it fully. I'm engaged, I'm present, and my interactions are genuine. I'm no longer reliant on some external stimulus to make things fun. I AM the fun.

I spent the first part of my life working hard to fit in, and the thought of even trying that now sounds exhausting. I no longer care about fitting in, especially if it means I have to get sloppy drunk to accomplish it. In fact, I'd rather *not* fit in. It sounds much sexier and more fun to do my own thing, follow my dreams, and focus on the things that fulfill me and make me happy. Going against the grain and loving it—that's peak adulthood. I'm happy to be an outlier and to share a different way of living. It feels a lot better than fitting in ever did.

I can't go back and undo my obsession with trying to conform when I was younger, just like I can't go back and un-drink all those gallons of cabernet. I *can* make sure I don't waste another minute of the rest of my life trying to stuff myself into a mold that isn't the right fit.

21

Sober is Boring, Right?

Early on, I felt good about my new, alcohol-free social life. My friends were supportive, and I was having fun. I felt secure in my ability to be around others who were drinking. It didn't bother me or feel like a trigger. Keep in mind that we were still in a global pandemic, so my social life wasn't comparable to pre-2020, but I still felt good about the number of events and activities I had enjoyed without alcohol.

Then, one Friday evening, I was home alone with my boys. The kiddos and I had planned a fun evening—our favorite Mexican takeout and an introduction to Ben Stiller films through Zoolander. While we waited for the food to arrive, I scrolled Instagram. I noticed a few good friends had new stories up, so I checked them out to see what everyone was up to. They were all together. And I was not with them. I put the pieces together in slow motion. They were having a girls' night at the wine bar up the street, which was my absolute favorite spot, drinking or not. My heart sank, and I felt incredibly sad. Why wasn't I invited? Did they think I wouldn't want to go, or it would make me uncomfortable? Or did they not want me there because sober Hadley is no fun? Did they talk about it? "Should we invite Hadley? She'd probably say no." Or did it not even occur to them? I couldn't decide which was worse.

Then I thought, "*Oh God*, what if it's because I talk about being sober all the time?" No one wants to listen to a sober friend babbling on about how great not drinking is while trying to down a bottle of pinot and put a long week behind them. I've turned into *that* person, ugh! I was sad, confused, and my feelings hurt on a cellular level.

After a few days of reflection, I decided it was okay to be sad, but also that it was my responsibility to communicate my needs to my friends. How else would they know how I felt? Maybe if I had proactively talked to them, I wouldn't have sat home on a Friday night wondering if I was suddenly *persona non grata*. Or maybe they genuinely didn't want me there, and I'd have to deal with that, too. Either way, becoming sober in a world that snubs its nose at sobriety can feel isolating and scary.

The world has conspired to teach us that drinking is an integral part of the human experience. Booze = fun, excitement, and glamour. Sober = boring, stick-in-the-mud, dull. We see these sentiments reinforced everywhere. "No good story ever starts with a salad!" Right?

Even the word "sober" sounds dull and unpleasant. "Lame" might be the best synonym. Being sober, in general, or at a particular event, isn't a desirable state. How on earth did we do that as a society? How did we turn the absence of intoxication by a *drug* into a negative thing with a stigma attached? It's bizarre when you think about it.

We learn early on that being sober is stodgy and uninteresting. Even if we never think or say those words specifically, we make our position clear in so many ways. "BOOO, why aren't you drinking?" or "Someone's going to be no fun tonight," or "Come on, don't you want to just have one?" Then there are the old standards: "sober as a judge" or "stone-cold sober." Those aren't labels that sound appealing. We seem to have accepted that being clear-headed and unimpaired is not sexy.

When you're newly sober, this can all seem very confusing, especially when you're in what we refer to as the "pink cloud" phase. Even though there's nothing easy about getting sober, you probably recognize that the world feels a little brighter. There's a little more joy and a lot less guilt and shame. There's a feeling of hope and excitement in the air. For a time, it feels almost magical.

Instead of thinking of the word "sober" with a negative connotation, I now look at it differently. Sober Hadley is full of joy and self-respect. She wakes up feeling confident and without fear over what might have happened the night before. She embraces each day with enthusiasm that isn't possible with a hangover. She feels sparkly, happy, and fun. Her laughter is genuine, not exaggerated and obnoxious. Sober Hadley will keep your secrets and remember our plans for next week. She's still learning how to do things like dance and sing karaoke without the ole' liquid courage, but she's getting there.

Let's start by changing the terminology. Instead of "sober as a judge," it should be "sober as a unicorn." Or "stone-cold sober" should be "sparkle pants sober." Something that conveys how damn good it feels while simultaneously busting the stigma and making it sound cool.

Ultimately, that's what I'd like to do: show people that choosing sobriety isn't lame or boring. It's exciting, courageous, and life-altering. Living alcohol-free is the sign of a leader, not a follower. Sobriety might not be for everyone, but those who choose to walk this path should feel confident that they aren't being looked down on. They should feel supported and respected, not like they're getting attacked from all angles.

22

Unlocking FUN After Booze

Learning to navigate the world without alcohol is like tiptoeing through a minefield. It's messy and rarely perfect. There might be some explosions along the way.

It took some practice to get to this point where I feel like life is beautiful and fulfilling on the other side. First, I had to work on myself through that combination of self-care, education, and community I've mentioned. Oh, yeah, and that work never ends. Then, I had to figure out what I wanted my social life to look like now that I was alcohol-free. I didn't experience physical withdrawal symptoms or have to detox when I quit drinking, but I had to detox from our boozy culture, which seems to consider drinking a mandatory part of adulthood.

In hindsight, I now realize I worked my way through three steps that helped me navigate being out in the world without booze as a buffer or crutch. They also helped me avoid hurt feelings and more situations like the girls' night I had been excluded from.

1. I analyzed the role alcohol had played in my social life.

When I confronted my relationship with alcohol, it also meant taking a hard look at my social life, how I spent my time, and who I spent it with. I realized how deeply connected drinking had become to everything I did. Dinner out with my husband or friends was synonymous with cocktails. Brunch meant mimosas. Book club meant red wine. A warm, sunny day meant day drinking was mandatory. Any social event, celebration, or gathering became all about alcohol. I *knew* I needed to unlink activities from alcohol in my mind to be successful at giving it up.

I considered the things I enjoy doing and who I enjoy doing them with. I admitted I don't like hanging out at noisy bars, clubs, or even concerts. My hearing impairment makes scenarios with lots of background noise miserable. Combine that with my introverted tendencies, and you'll never hear sober Hadley say, "I want to go dancing," or "Let's go to a party." It's not my jam. I only tolerated those things so I wouldn't miss out on anything, and I only tolerated them with *lots* of booze. It was so liberating to stop pretending and to cut those things from my life.

I prefer quiet time with close friends in smaller groups where we're talking, laughing, and *doing* things. I love dinners out with good food and going for a walk or run with friends. I enjoy activities like hiking, bowling, or playing pickleball. I would much rather get a pedicure with a friend than meet people at a busy brewery on Saturday night. I want to talk, laugh, and spend time with the people I enjoy. Alcohol doesn't need to be a part of that. Honestly, it's all more fun sober! I remember everything; I don't lose my phone, and there is zero shame the next day. I'm a better listener and a better friend.

I also took a hard look at my friendships and the different groups I spent time with. I had to face the truth that some people weren't a good fit. If I took drinking out of the equation, would I want to spend time with them? Could I picture explaining my decision to stop drinking and inviting them to go on a sober hike with me? Did I think they would support this change in my life? If not, then it was probably time to bless and release.

I spent a lot of my life trying to fit in with the cool crowd and thinking that alcohol was my entry ticket. It's too bad it took me until I was over forty to realize I didn't need to work to fit in with the right people. The right people love us for who we are, with or without alcohol. Life is way too short to do crap you don't like with people you don't enjoy and having to be drunk so you can tolerate it.

This is where I encourage you to look at your own social life and think about these things. How do you most commonly spend your free time, and is alcohol a big part? Look back at your calendar for the past month and review everything you've done for fun. How many of those events involved drinking? Think about those gatherings or events and decide whether they brought you joy, or is the next day's hangover what you remember most? The very first feeling or thought that comes to mind is probably the truest one. Did you truly enjoy yourself, or was it just a booze fest? What people did you have the most fun with, and who do you think would support your desire to make a change?

Maybe you're my opposite—a total extrovert. Maybe you *love* concerts, big events, and bars. Perhaps you live for some good karaoke and a crowd. That's fine. The point is to come up with a list of what you genuinely enjoy. Do the same thing with people. Who are the people you most enjoy spending time with, and does that list change if you remove alcohol from the equation?

Working through this exercise helped me figure out where I wanted to spend my time and who I wanted to spend it with!

2. I created boundaries

When I first eliminated alcohol, I had it easy for a while. We were still in the pandemic, and Eric had a compromised immune system, so we were pretty isolated. That allowed me to tackle my demons in private first before really going back out into the world. When everything opened back up, I missed my friends, and I was excited to do things, but I hadn't thought about how my new, alcohol-free life would work. I told all my friends I wasn't drinking, and they seemed supportive, but in hindsight, I'm not sure they believed me yet.

Then, when I realized my friends weren't inviting me places, I was confused and frustrated. I wondered what I had done wrong. I didn't realize I needed boundaries to help me navigate this new world successfully. Would I have actually gone if they had invited me to some of these things, or did I just want to be asked? I wasn't sure, but it prompted me to make a list that went something like this:

Please still invite me places, even if sometimes I say no.

I don't care if everyone else is drinking. It rarely bothers me, but I reserve the right to bail early if it becomes too much.

I would love it if we could plan occasional activities that don't revolve around alcohol.

*I promise I'm not judging you for drinking. My
decision was about me and no one else.*

*If I talk about my sobriety a lot, that's because
it's the most significant thing in my life right
now. I'm not trying to convert you.*

*I don't mind being the designated driver sometimes, but I won't
be closing down the bars, and I might want to leave early.*

*I will need a separate check when we're out so I don't split a
bill with four bottles of wine and a round of fireball shots.*

*I'm still the same fun Hadley. In fact, I
think I'm even more fun now.*

*If you're unsure whether I want to do something,
please ask me, and I'll tell you.*

This list was a first crack at my sober boundaries. These will look different for everyone, and they are deeply personal. They're important because they'll keep you on track through the ups and downs. It's okay if your boundaries change. There are no right or wrong answers here.

You'll need to consider whether you can be around drinking at all, and it's okay if you can't. I don't mind it up to a point, but if people get wasted, I reserve the right to duck out early without saying goodbye. Can you be at a bar or club, or would you rather avoid them altogether? If friends come to your house, are you okay if they bring wine, or is that a hard no? Are you all right being a designated driver, or would you rather not be trapped staying late?

You'll need to think about what triggers you, what makes you uncomfortable, and what might jeopardize your promise to yourself. You'll need to decide how you feel about non-alcoholic beverages, which have blown up in popularity recently. It's fabulous that the NA options are multiplying, but fake whiskey is not okay for everyone. If that's a trigger for you, but your friend has graciously bought some to have for you at their party, be ready to stand by that boundary and say, "No thanks."

I encourage you to sit down and make a list of these things. Come up with your own alcohol-free bill of rights. It's up to you what you do with this list, but it will be great to have and update over time.

Boundaries will look different for each of us. They can be fluid; they aren't fixed. Most importantly, they are *yours*. They exist to keep you comfortable and help you succeed with the changes you want to make. This is just a starting point to build from. You might not be ready to answer some of these questions if you're just thinking about making a change, but you'll get there. In fact, you'll be ahead of the game.

3. I made a plan to curate a more fulfilling social life

I started thinking of my social life like the old food pyramid we used to learn about in school. What was at the base or foundation? Was my pyramid built on solid, fulfilling friendships and activities that fueled my soul and made me happy? Were fun cocktails sprinkled in toward the tippy top of that pyramid, or did mimosa brunches and afternoons at the winery with superficial friends make up the foundation? Thinking of it that way helped me envision what my ideal social life would look like.

I wanted to fill that big bottom layer with friends and family who respect me and my choices—people who want to see me happy, healthy, thriving, and vice versa. I wanted the next layer to be made up of the things I enjoy doing. Not getting wasted at bars, but enjoying my hobbies and the things that bring me joy. This is where it might look different for everyone. For me, it's running, playing pickleball, hiking, etc. It's quality time with people I enjoy. Then, as the pyramid narrows up, I will sprinkle in special occasions like great food, dinners out, coffee dates, movies, and sporting events. Concerts and anywhere loud or crowded would be at the narrow top of my social life pyramid because they're not where I prefer to spend my time.

Think about your pyramid and consider what changes you need to make. If you're already spending your time with the things and people that make up the base layers of your pyramid, it should be a lot easier to drink less. Those are the people and activities that are most fulfilling to you. Recall the list of boundaries you created and decide how they stack up against that pyramid. If you've decided you can't be at bars or around others who are drinking, then make sure those activities are nowhere on your pyramid.

This step prompted me to talk to my friends and family openly. I was honest that I didn't know exactly what I needed yet or how it would all unfold, but I told them about some of the boundaries I'd created and asked for support. I knew the people I was comfortable having this conversation with were those who mattered. It's not easy, but if we're going to make a significant change like this, we need to practice advocating for ourselves. We're going to have to speak up for ourselves a lot.

Since making these changes, I've started meeting a few friends for walks to catch up. I go to lunch with someone different once a week. A crew of close friends plays pickleball once or twice a week, and we're on a mission to try every taco joint in the DC area. I've gone to lots of dinners out, and when I made it clear that I needed a separate check, no one even batted an eye. I've gone axe throwing and had game nights and adventures with my family. I wasn't thinking about what I would drink or how many I should have. I was present and engaged and having a blast.

My close friends don't just accept my choices—they respect them. We love and support one another. Do you know what the best part is? I still laugh *just as hard* when I'm with them as I did when I was two glasses of pinot deep. I'm still introverted, but my close friends, the people who matter, already know that and accept it. I don't need alcohol to erase my inhibitions for me to socialize. If everyone else is drinking, they certainly will not notice any awkwardness I might feel.

I've made a conscious decision to live out of the wide bottom half of my social life pyramid. As a result, my relationships have grown deeper and more authentic. I remember our conversations, and I'm a better friend. I'm better at honoring myself and my boundaries and at saying no to people and situations that don't feel right.

It's not all sunshine and roses. People will ask annoying questions about why I don't drink or make patronizing comments. There will be some who are rude or obnoxious, but usually, that's a sign that they're struggling with their own relationship with alcohol.

It won't *always* be easy. Even on the hard days, I know I'm on the right path, and I'm never turning back.

23

Deprive or Thrive

The rallying cry of the wellness industry in this new anti-diet culture era is "YOU DON'T HAVE TO DEPRIVE YOURSELF TO BE HEALTHY!" The idea is that you shouldn't have to give up the things you love to lose weight or meet some unrealistic ideal. I agree, and I'm here for it, but this concept has grown beyond the idea of enjoying the food you love without guilt and turned into an excuse to drink alcohol freely.

People all over the internet are touting their fitness and nutrition regimens and shouting from the rooftops that you don't have to give up your wine, beer, or martinis to get fit and healthy. People viciously defend their stance on allowing alcohol as part of their healthy lifestyle. I get it because I used to be that person. I would never have suggested that my clients eliminate alcohol to meet their goals. "That would be unrealistic," I'd tell them. "Just use moderation!" It was hilarious advice coming from me.

Can you drink alcohol and also be ripped with a six-pack? Sure! Can you drink and still be generally healthy and fit? Of course! I'm not saying the two are always mutually exclusive. But many of us are sabotaging our healthy efforts with a quantity of alcohol that's hurting us in several ways. Alcohol and wellness simply don't belong in the same conversation, and the evidence is now showing that even small amounts have negative consequences.

No number of organic beet smoothies and lunges will negate drinking wine most nights of the week. Your body can't run at peak performance when you flood it with something it recognizes as poison. It has to work hard to compensate and detox. By the time it recovers, the cycle starts all over again. Sorry to burst our collective champagne bubble, but in a world where everyone wants to be "healthy," that will not cut it.

There's a difference between refusing to give up chocolate or carbs to meet your health goals and refusing to give up ten or twenty drinks a week. One is an example of a reasonable boundary, while the other is rationalizing the use of a toxic, addictive substance.

What if I told you this all boiled down to a simple mindset shift? *What if* we thought of it differently? We're not depriving ourselves when we choose not to drink; we're allowing ourselves to thrive. Without alcohol pumping through our system, we can give our bodies a fighting chance to get and stay healthy.

I'm the perfect example of this shift in thinking. Until I quit drinking, I was convinced alcohol would and should always be a part of my life. No way would I give it up! I deserved it, and I would not deprive myself. I was super healthy, dammit, and I shouldn't have to give up something I loved!

Let's look at what was going on with my body, though. I was constantly tired and suffering from intense anxiety, regular depressive episodes, and crazy gut issues. I worked hard on running goals, but I kept getting injured and made little progress. I had a raging hangover at least once a week, my sleep quality was horrible, and I always felt rundown.

When I finally decided enough was enough and pulled the plug, I didn't feel deprived or cheated. I felt an overwhelming sense of freedom. I felt healthy. My sleep improved, my skin improved, and my running performance improved. It was life-changing in so many ways. It makes me cringe to think of how long I fought for and clung to the idea that I needed to keep alcohol in my life.

I'm not insisting everyone needs to walk away cold turkey. I'm only suggesting there are likely many others, like me, who probably need a nudge to look honestly at how much they're consuming and think about the impact on their physical and mental health. We're very good at lying to ourselves—I certainly was.

I still won't cut chocolate or carbs from my life because that would be crazy, but I'm damn glad I finally cut the booze. I feel truly healthy, inside and out, for the first time in ages. The fitness/booze paradox is one that I'll no longer take part in.

24

Exercise Gives Us Superpowers

I've been running since I was twelve, and while I've always loved it, its significance in my life has shifted like the tides. In my first year of high school, I went out for the cross-country team and excelled, earning my varsity letter as a freshman. I returned for my sophomore year, but my heart wasn't in it. I had no interest in hard work and early morning practices once I was partying. I hurt my knee toward the end of the season, likely a product of my shabby training habits and lack of commitment, and I used that minor injury as an excuse to walk away. It pains me that I casually tossed aside something I was great at because I didn't want it to interfere with my social life. It's hard not to wonder what might have been. Where might the sport have taken me if I hadn't stumbled into booze? Maybe I'd be one of the elite runners I now love to cheer for.

I continued to run on and off through college and beyond, but I viewed it solely as a tool to manage my body. I did it purely for weight loss, not for the joy of running. It's ironic, since now, as a seasoned runner, I know running is not a great tool for weight loss.

After college, I fell back in love with running for all the right reasons. I learned to enjoy the feeling in my legs and lungs as I stretched my limits. Running became a part of me. It made me feel alive.

When my sons were born, my reasons shifted again. Running became a way to stay in touch with who I'd been before becoming a mom. It was a way to challenge myself. It made me feel strong and confident when I struggled with my identity. It also gave me independence and a chance to get some much-needed alone time. Running allowed me to clear my mind, and it kept me from losing my shit as I experienced depression for the first time. It became a critical part of my self-care toolkit.

I never believed I was an athlete, and I joked about my lack of grace and coordination. With running, I discovered I was capable of more than I realized. When I ran my first marathon in under four hours, it confirmed that I was, in fact, a damn good runner. Running 26.2 miles is a challenge that's difficult to put into words. You can prepare as much as possible for the physical aspect of the race, but the mental challenge is equally extreme. It pushes you to your limits, and the feeling after you succeed is a special kind of high.

From that point on, I moved through different seasons of running. Some seasons were more about a sense of community and the friends I ran with. Some aligned with difficult life seasons, and running was a critical part of my coping strategy. When I lost my hearing suddenly and inexplicably in the summer of 2015, I was in a marathon training cycle. It was a scary time, and it would have been easy to throw up my hands and give up on my goals. It would have been understandable if I had pulled out of the race amid all the doctors' visits and an unpleasant prognosis. Instead, I leaned into my training, and my runs became my therapy. I ran countless miles with tears streaming down my face as I wondered if I'd be entirely deaf and unable to hear my sweet boys' voices. I debated the pros and cons of different hearing aid solutions as I pounded the pavement. I stumbled along, trying to listen for bikes passing behind me on the trail and positioning myself so I could best hear my running partner next to me. It was a period full of unknowns and tough decisions, but running kept me sharp and sane.

Despite all the positives it brought me, my running often collided messily with my drinking.

I have vivid memories of a miserable ten-mile run with a friend one Sunday morning after a rowdy neighborhood party. We had each finished a bottle of wine the night before, and we laughed as we ran, joking about how awful we felt as we slugged through the miles. When we finished, I was shaky and nauseous. I'm sure I considered it a successful run, but nothing about it was successful. Those miles accomplished nothing but taxing my already struggling body, putting my organs into panic mode.

There were plenty of other runs just like that one over the years. I even made a glass of red wine (or two) a non-negotiable part of my pre-race meal the night before, regardless of the distance I was running. You know, to relax me so I could get to sleep more easily.

I ignored the cues my body was sending as my drinking escalated. I fought to run through hangovers on little sleep and inadequate nutrition. I operated under the assumption that "sweating it out" was a viable solution and "mind over matter" was the answer to everything.

When I stopped drinking, running became a key pillar of my sobriety. It gave me something productive to focus on. It gave me space to process my thoughts, and it allowed me to blow off steam and channel my emotions into something that made me feel alive and vibrant. I noticed a significant difference in my performance and recovery now that I was sleeping well, fueling well, and treating my body kindly. It made me want to see what I could accomplish as a runner over forty. If I could be a decent runner while slowly pickling myself with red wine, what could I do now that I was sober and healthy?

My first alcohol-free year saw my highest mileage ever, and in addition to my body feeling healthy and strong, my thinking during runs is so much more productive now. I spent so much of my running time agonizing over my drinking regrets and stewing in shame. Now, there's nothing left to agonize over, and I can focus on more important things. You spend a lot of time in your own head as a runner, and if your headspace is messy and not well-tended, that can be a tough place to be.

I'm a better runner because I'm alcohol-free, and I'm better at being alcohol-free because I'm a runner. The two have gone well together, and I can't wait to see how my running career unfolds over the next few years. I expect my reasons for loving the sport will evolve, but I know it will always be an essential part of my life.

I'm lucky to love exercise because not everyone does. If you're someone who wants to gag at the thought of an hour at the gym, hang in there. You can still reap the rewards of exercise even if the idea of getting your sweat on doesn't make you want to hop out of bed in the morning. I genuinely believe that anyone can learn to enjoy and appreciate (or at least tolerate) exercise and all its benefits. There's something out there for everyone.

Exercise teaches us so many life lessons, and we can harness these lessons into what I call superpowers.

Exercise encourages us to push our limits and shows us we're stronger than we realize. It builds confidence and resilience, and it empowers us. We learn how to set goals and go after them, even when we want to quit. It gets us out of our comfort zone. We begin to believe in ourselves. That's in addition to the well-documented physical benefits—a stronger body, a more efficient heart, and stronger bones. Exercise also improves our mood, boosts energy, and promotes better sleep and brain health.

Those superpowers will bleed over into all aspects of our lives and help us tackle whatever challenges life throws us. They can definitely support us as we change our relationship with alcohol.

There's another significant perk to keep in mind. If you've seen the movie *Legally Blonde*, you know that "Exercise gives us endorphins, endorphins make us happy, and happy people don't kill their husbands." That might be extreme, but you get the point. Maybe it's that happy people don't feel the need to drown themselves in chardonnay or drink until they black out and wake up with major hang-xiety. The evidence shows that exercise's mood-boosting properties are significant. Exercise also reduces levels of the body's stress hormones, such as adrenaline and cortisol. All of this is good news for anyone thinking about dialing back on the booze.

A great article by Harvard Health talks about exercise's unique ability to relax us, calm us, dissipate stress, and counteract depression.[1] It explains the neurochemical basis for all of this. That runner's high you hear about, it's a real thing. This article promises that just about any kind of exercise can help.

It doesn't matter if you've ever enjoyed exercise or done it consistently. If you want to change your relationship with alcohol, moving your body will be an essential tool in your toolbox. It will help you physically and mentally as you work through your baggage. That doesn't mean you need to start an extreme fitness regimen or sign up for a marathon. It *does* mean you should look for ways to build more consistent exercise habits. Look for things you enjoy (or tolerate) and work them into your life until you've created habits that will stick. At the very least, get outside and go for a walk. Breathing fresh air while you move your body has amazing benefits.

Waiting for some magical bolt of motivation to strike before you start rarely works. Act first, and the motivation will follow. The secret miracle of motivation is that it doesn't show up until you start moving … then you will feel motivated, excited, and confident.

I'm rarely motivated to wake up and put in the work at five in the morning, but I do it because I've cultivated discipline and developed lasting habits. I know once I get moving and the blood starts pumping, that motivation will kick in, and I'll be glad I did it.

Movement is medicine. If we actively look for more ways to move our bodies, it will pay off in countless ways, especially if we're thinking about addressing booze in our lives. Changing your relationship with alcohol is tough, so why not arm yourself with as many superpowers as possible before you tackle it?

25

Boozy Role Models

Before my last big race, an athlete I long admired and respected announced a partnership with a big beer company. The first video I saw showed her, presumably, coming back from a workout and opening a refrigerator full of beer. She grabbed one and started swigging like it was the perfect post-workout thirst quencher.

I caught myself feeling shocked, icky, and disappointed as I watched it unfold on social media for millions to see. I was a little embarrassed by how visceral my reaction was. When I quit drinking, I swore I wasn't on some kind of crusade to banish booze from the world. I cringed, thinking, "Oh geez, now I'm turning into the crazy, prudish, sober lady!"

An elite athlete conveying the message that a fridge full of beer is part of a healthy lifestyle sends a fascinating message to women out there. First of all, I call BS because there's no way an athlete of her caliber isn't rushing home to eat a well-balanced meal of carbs and protein after strenuous workouts. There's no way her nutrition isn't dialed in with scientific precision, and there's no way she's drinking a whole fridge full of beer while she's training at that level. Bullllshittttt!

My immediate reaction was that I wanted to unfollow her,

thinking, "Well, she lost someone who used to be a loyal fan and an emphatic cheerleader." I stopped myself because, even though I felt let down, I also felt like I was being really judgy. In her profession, it's pretty tough to make money, so maybe she's got to take the opportunities that come her way. I tried to think about what the old me would have done if faced with stacks of cash to endorse a beer brand, and I honestly don't know.

I'm sure this particular athlete had no idea her partnership would ruffle feathers, or maybe she just didn't care. As someone who likely drinks a beer now and then, she may have no clue how many women struggle with alcohol. She doesn't get how damaging a message like hers can be to those most susceptible to the narrative Big Alcohol has created for us.

Big Alcohol is brilliant. They have figured out how to market to women, and it works. It works so well that it has created an epidemic of alcohol use disorders and women who desperately wish they could cut back. The booze industry has also figured out how to pit us against each other, and we don't realize we're doing it. "Want to be prettier, sexier, faster, stronger, more desirable, more worthy? Alcohol can give you all that and more. Just look at this woman you admire who has what *you* want. Doesn't she look sophisticated and chic with that glass of wine or fancy cocktail? She can drink beer and run a five-minute mile."

Since I first saw my beloved athlete strike up a partnership with that beer company, it has become clear that said company is on a mission to drill deep into the market of female runners. We are a target market, and they're coming after us with a vengeance. The 2022 New York City Marathon was the week before I was set to run my first marathon since ditching booze, and social media was exploding with content from runners, both elite and every day, partnering with this same beer brand. The company expertly crafted a campaign promoting equality and diversity in the sport, which clearly got the participating athletes excited to link arms with them. One entire team of women ran the race with the beer company's logo drawn on their arms in Sharpie ink.

Messages like this tell us that drinking is normal, everyone does it, and everyone *should* do it. These messages tell us that a beer after a run is a great way to replenish carbs and celebrate what you just accomplished. Beer is a reward, and we deserve it. As a runner, this phenomenon at races has baffled me for as long as I can remember. Even when I was an enthusiastic drinker, I couldn't imagine cashing in my free beer ticket after running 26.2 miles.

These messages also suggest (promise?) that we should be able to drink with no issues. We're to blame if there is a problem, not the product. Meanwhile, countless people are struggling with alcohol in some capacity. Lives and families have been ruined, futures destroyed, and potential wasted. It's still marketed like some luxury product instead of a drug and known carcinogen.

One week after I watched this alcohol theme unfold at the NYC Marathon, I toed the line to run 26.2 in Richmond. Either the drinking theme at my race was more intense than ever, or I was just more aware of it through my newly sober eyes. During the race, I saw at least fifteen spectator signs encouraging us that we were almost done running so we could start drinking. I saw a mini mimosa stand where people were handing out champagne and OJ to runners. One person was distributing fireball shots to athletes. I saw people handing out White Claw and beers from a cooler along the course. I was shocked by how many runners were accepting these drinks with laughter and cheers.

This was an unseasonably hot November race. It was seventy-five degrees with high humidity, and the sun was blazing. The running conditions were less than ideal for a fall race. Staying well-hydrated was critical, and even with a laser focus on my water intake and electrolyte balance, I got the hot chills and was fighting back vomit by mile twenty-three. People were dropping like flies from heat stroke. I can't imagine how I would have felt or what might have happened if I had been taking shots along the way or chugging mimosas. Marathons are an amazing test of strength and perseverance, and they are tough on your body. Alcohol is the absolute last thing you need when you're pushing yourself to your limit. I can't comprehend how we accept drinking as a complement to intense physical activity.

Alcohol is the opposite of what athletes need—before, during, or after a race or training session. That's not just my opinion; it's literally science. It's another example of how Big Alcohol has tricked us by weaving a perceived need for alcohol into the everyday fabric of our lives, whether or not it makes sense.

I'm not suggesting athletes shouldn't ever have a drink from time to time as part of a balanced lifestyle. But there's a huge difference between enjoying a drink periodically and promoting a beer brand like it's the key to a successful training regimen. I wish we could abolish the predatory tactical marketing strategies designed to hit women where we are the weakest. Let's call it a truce.

Big Alcohol, you tapped into our demographic and won, fair and square. It was a tough fight, but you were clearly up for the challenge. You beat us into submission and got more of us drinking than ever before. You convinced us that drinking is necessary, glamorous, and sexy. It's the hallmark of the modern, independent woman. You've made a lot of money from us along the way—*a lot*. Now fuck off!

We're done rolling over and are ready to fight back. Right, ladies? It's time for us to tell Big Alcohol where to stick their "Mommy Juice" and targeted ad campaigns. It's time for us to stop letting them convince us we need alcohol to cope with the chaotic demands of womanhood. We can and should figure this out and make our own decisions without allowing any more of their influence.

Let's rebuild and rally to help the women who didn't escape their toxic marketing campaigns unscathed. Let us collectively recognize that alcohol is the problem and no longer blame the women who fell victim to the sexy promises they so expertly engineered. Let's tell a more realistic story about what alcohol does. Let's share the reality of it instead of the fantasy. Let us work together instead of sitting back and letting them use us against each other to strengthen their bottom lines.

Women are unbelievably strong and intelligent, and I know we can figure this out—together. We need to work harder as a gender to support and uplift each other. We are responsible for recognizing when we're being preyed upon, and we must refuse to be a part of it. Whether you drink or not, you can still say NO to being part of the problem. You can stand up and be part of the solution instead.

We're up for the challenge. I know it.

26

Sober in Paradise

I was cranky and on edge when we first arrived at the resort in Punta Cana, Dominican Republic. Servers bearing trays of cocktails were circulating the check-in line, and everyone was grabbing them with gusto. I tried to order something alcohol-free, but the language barrier and lack of options made it impossible. I rolled my eyes and growled, "Never mind!" I felt edgy and frustrated as my husband tossed back his first few drinks. My thoughts spiraled. "I'm not going to have any fun," "I'm already annoyed," and "Why did I think I could do this?"

As we navigated the confusing check-in process, my husband and I did that thing married couples often do in these situations. We got snappy and started griping at each other. We huffed and puffed as we figured out where to go. When we finally got to our beautiful suite, I looked around and took a deep breath. I knew I needed to let go of all the stress and tension and breathe in some ocean air ASAP. We headed out to explore the pools and beach, and I felt the negativity slowly leave my body, but I knew it would take a conscious effort to let it all go.

I struggled to get into vacay mode for the rest of the evening. I couldn't figure out what had me on edge, but I caught myself grumbling and rolling my eyes every time my husband looked for a bartender. I had a short fuse, and everything was setting it off. After a welcome reception on the beach, we ended up at the putt-putt golf course with a friend and her family. Eric offered to play with the kids so we could sit and catch up, if I found him a drink first. I thought my head might blow off. "I am not going to wander around this resort in the dark trying to find a bar because you need a drink to play mini golf with our kids." I was fuming and convinced I would *hate* every second of this trip.

This vacation was a big deal for many reasons, and we'd been looking forward to it for ages. This was a trip I earned through my coaching business, meaning it was essentially free and a reward for a year of hard work. Considering that for the past two years, the trip had been canceled because of COVID, it was more like a reward for three years' worth of hard work. My boys had been on two of these trips with us in the past and had a blast. They recognized these opportunities resulted from the blood, sweat, and tears they saw me pouring into my fitness business. It felt amazing to give them these experiences and to know they were proud of me for my hard work.

This was also the first vacation, probably since my teenage years, where I would be alcohol-free. I was excited but nervous because alcohol is a big part of the all-inclusive resort experience, and I did not know what it would be like to navigate one sober.

Usually, a trip like this would go as follows: drinks on the plane, mimosas with breakfast, daiquiris by the pool, beers on the beach, cocktails in the afternoon, and wine at dinner. Start early, repeat often, and get your money's worth. I would inevitably fall asleep by the pool or in the room and feel foggy and hungover by dinner. I would spend mornings trying to hydrate or sweat out the day's hangover. I wouldn't be fully present with my kids because I was too focused on the drinking itinerary. Not that I was ever fully drunk when we were traveling as a family, but drinking still took up an embarrassing amount of mental space. That's what vacations were all about—no rules and a chance to let loose and unwind (i.e., drink as much as you want).

This notion was reinforced the week before the trip when the text thread with our friends joining us on the trip started blowing up. We coordinated travel itineraries, outfits, and plans, when the subject somehow switched to drinking. I sat and read the exchange with a pit in my stomach as everyone talked about how excited they were to party and how to best maximize their drinking and minimize hangovers. They strategized about what time to start and stop drinking, how much water to drink and when, and how to space the Liquid IV and ibuprofen to ensure they didn't puke and could still get up for the group workouts each morning. Reading the texts took me back to the days when I would wake up with a dry mouth and the spins, feeling like death but not wanting to waste a day in paradise. That was how I had spent so many previous vacations, and I was happy I wouldn't have to worry about it this time. It sounded like a horrible way to spend the trip. I wasn't judging them for their desire to party, but I was relieved that I wouldn't have to worry about any of that.

The exchange still brought up so many questions. Would I still have fun? Would I feel left out? How would I feel about my husband drinking?

I was also jealous. At that point, early on, it still sometimes pissed me off that I couldn't enjoy a mojito by the pool or a glass of red wine with my steak dinner. It was infuriating that I couldn't—well, *wouldn't*—let loose with some cocktails for one night on vacation and cut myself off before it went too far. Sometimes it just felt *so* damn unfair. Why the hell couldn't I moderate like a normal person? Why didn't I get to have some fun drinks in the sun like everyone else? Why did I have to quit drinking altogether? I would probably be fine just having a few, right?

I had a feeling that sentiment might intensify on a trip like this, even if it was irrational. When I stopped and took a deep breath, I knew better. I was throwing myself a little pity party. I know that moderation will never be my jam. I'm an all-or-nothing gal, and my life is much better when I choose "nothing." The "all" option has burned me time and time again. It's not a question of fairness; it's a choice. A choice that allows me to be the person I'm meant to be, live the life I want to live, and feel good about myself. The universe is not out to get me by denying me the privilege of moderate drinking. Alcohol is an addictive, carcinogenic substance that doesn't work for me. That's not unfair; it's science.

By the time I woke up the following day, I felt like a new person. The stress, anger, and frustration had dissipated, and I was ready to have fun *my* way. I decided it was up to me to enjoy myself, and I remembered that not drinking would have so many benefits. I felt like a million bucks as I headed to my first outdoor group workout of the week and thought about how gross I would feel if I had been drinking the night before. That was enough to put a smile on my face for the rest of the morning.

I watched everyone else drink and party for the rest of the trip, and it didn't bother me one bit. We enjoyed a great balance of family time and time with friends, and it all just worked. My friends and their husbands respected my choice not to drink and brought me alcohol-free drinks at the bar. It was empowering to know that they had my back and didn't care, just like I didn't care that they were drinking. In some crowds, you feel uncomfortable or like you need to explain yourself and offer excuses.

Instead, they made me feel relaxed and confident. There were no snide remarks, eye rolls, or awkward questions—just unwavering support and respect.

By the last day, I evaluated all the benefits of not drinking and realized how different this week felt from so many others like it. I wasn't bloated and feeling gross; I was getting ten (T-E-N!) quality hours of sleep a night, I was rested and relaxed, and the only Advil I had taken was so I could walk after a killer leg workout. I remembered every minute of the trip and didn't worry about whether I'd done anything stupid.

I loved being present with my kids and not distracted by drinking. Most of all, I loved that the boys saw me choosing not to drink in a place where everyone else was spending so much time and energy fixated on alcohol consumption. I felt proud to be setting that example and showing a different option. We picked different alcohol-free drinks to try together and sniffed them before we sipped to ensure the servers hadn't messed up. I enjoyed soft-serve ice cream by the pool with them several times a day because, *shit*, think of the calories I was saving!

Like so many other firsts I've experienced since I quit drinking, this alcohol-free vacation turned out to be beautiful and uplifting. Before, I thought drinking was essential to a fun vacation, but my entire week was more vibrant and authentic without it.

I didn't feel left out, or like I was missing anything by not hanging at the nightspots with our friends after dinner each night. I laughed as I heard stories the next day about the trouble they'd gotten into, and I was grateful not to feel any of the shame I would have felt if I'd been taking part in the craziness. The time I spent with everyone during the day was quality time. The only thing I missed out on was drunk time when no real connection was happening.

When our plane from Punta Cana landed in DC after a magical week of fun in the sun, we walked out of the airport into thirty-five-degree weather and wanted to cry as we drove home with blustery snowflakes swirling around the car. Re-entry is a bitch, but the memories of my first sober vacation linger.

27

Daydreaming About My Sobriety

At times, I think about alcohol and my sobriety a lot, and other times I go weeks without giving it a passing thought. There were times, in the beginning, when I felt I was grieving a loss. In a way, I was. I grieved the loss of something I considered critical to my lifestyle and happiness. I had made my love of wine a pillar of my freaking personality. Giving it up felt like an immense sacrifice at first.

Early on, I asked my husband, who has always been incredibly supportive, how he felt about my decision to stop drinking. He said it made him a little sad that we would never go to a winery together the way we used to. No more tastings and then enjoying a bottle over a baguette and cheese overlooking the rolling Virginia wine country hills. "*Yes!*" I whined. "That part makes me so sad, too!" It was like a punch to the gut. I loved that part of drinking. The experience of tasting good wine, sitting outside on a beautiful day, and enjoying a glass (okay, a bottle) of my favorite red. That had always been one of my favorite activities.

Then I thought through a few of the days we'd spent at wineries and inwardly groaned. Many of the winery tours with Eric and our friends I don't remember parts of because we got so trashed. We would rent a limo, and by the third or fourth winery of the day, we were all sloppy drunk. I don't remember getting home from a Mother's Day wine tour, but I do remember waking up the next morning still wearing my sunglasses. One extra-classy day, we all peed in a field because the line for the bathrooms was too long. Another time, we paid our twenty-year-old to be our church group's winery tour driver. By the last stop, he hung his head out the car window because the smell of wine was so strong he wanted to gag.

Then there were the tamer times when Eric and I would go alone on a date. After two or three glasses of wine, all I could do was fall asleep for the rest of the day until I woke at one in the morning with the spins and a hangover. We rambled on to each other a lot as we sipped and ate cheese, but I don't remember what we talked about.

I thought about what I enjoyed from those outings, and it had little to do with the wine. I liked being with my husband in a beautiful spot in beautiful weather. I liked sitting outside, talking, and enjoying each other's company. I liked being out with friends, eating good food, and connecting. Honestly, I could have done all that with a glass of club soda, and I would have enjoyed myself even more. I would remember everything. I would have spent that time genuinely connecting with the people I love instead of drunk babbling. I wouldn't feel any shame from blacking out or getting sloppy drunk.

So much of what I thought I was sacrificing has turned out to be a blessing. I thought I was giving up such a big piece of myself, but I was gaining so much in return. When I catch myself contemplating my sobriety, it's more from a place of gratitude. I'm grateful I made this change before things got worse. I'm thankful I learned how much better life could be alcohol-free. I'm grateful I realized it all when I did.

I'll never know if I would have spiraled further, finally hitting some version of rock bottom. Maybe I would have drifted along in that gray area, knowing I was operating at fifty percent but never getting quite bad enough to set off any warning bells. Maybe I would have gone through the rest of my life not knowing how good I was meant to feel. I'll always be grateful I fought my way out of that rut and quit trying to justify alcohol's place in my life.

Every new experience without alcohol is a milestone I want to celebrate. Each new scenario I navigate sober is a big win. Every party, special occasion, or vacation where I have a blast without booze makes me want to jump up and down. I'm not trying to convert the world to my sober life. It's just hard to keep it to myself when I feel like I've unlocked one of life's big secrets.

28

A New Normal

One snowy day during my freshman year of high school, we lucked out with a two-hour delay. My friends decided it was a great excuse to meet at someone's house for vodka and Sunny D screwdrivers before getting on the bus. Solid plan. My first-period class was English, and I had the most beloved teacher in the entire school. I thought I was playing it off well, but she took one look at me that morning and knew I was buzzed.

I asked to go to the bathroom, which was across the hall from our classroom. When I came out of the stall, I was terrified to see her waiting for me. I'll never forget what happened next. She grabbed my shoulders, looked into my eyes, and said, "Hadley, you are a pretty, blonde, white girl with everything in the world going for you. Don't you dare do something stupid and screw that up." I choked on my tongue a bit, nodded my head, and said, "Yes, ma'am." She returned to our classroom, and I took a minute to pull myself together. Then, I went back to class and got to work. She didn't report me, and we never spoke of it again. I'd love to say I never drank after that, but that would be BS. I can say that I never drank at, during, or before school again. After that, I was no angel, but I got my act together, got excellent grades, and was much more discrete with my transgressions.

It was years before I realized the magnitude of the lesson she hoped to teach me that day. She shared a lesson about white privilege while trying to save me from myself and my stupidity. That was heavy stuff for a drunk freshman in first-period English, but now I recognize it as the gift it was.

My drinking habits were considered normal, which by now should seem disturbing. By "normal," I mean not out of the ordinary, not regarded as extreme or troubling, and not raising any red flags. I drank in situations where I was expected to drink, and my behavior aligned with those around me. When I looked up the definition of "normal," I found "conforming to a standard; usual, typical, or expected." That sounds about right. The same people who had been binge-drinking in high school and college were now doing it in the backyard while watching the baby monitor in case the kids woke up. We were still chugging it by the bottle, but it was considered "classy" now that we were drinking good wine and wearing expensive clothes.

Unless they could see what was happening inside my booze-soaked brain, no one close to me would believe I had a problem. In our alcohol-centric culture, my behavior wasn't an outlier, and I worried people would judge me and think it had been worse than it was. Would they wonder if I'd been drunk at the kids' sporting events and hiding airplane bottles in my purse during church meetings? I took a deep breath and decided not to care what people thought about me and my drinking once I shared my story.

I felt enough shame during my drinking career. I refuse to feel shame now that I've quit. I know there are many others stuck in the gray area like I was, with unhealthy but "normal" drinking habits they're struggling to reconcile. Like these:

Drinking until you puke

Blacking out and not remembering entire nights or chunks of nights

Waking up and not knowing how you got home

Drinking to get drunk

Making sexual decisions you would not have made sober

A hangover that lasts for a week

Funneling or shot-gunning beers to get drunk faster

Regularly feeling shame, anxiety, fear, and self-loathing

Spending more money on drinks than you can afford

Worrying that you made someone angry or that someone's mad at you

Not wanting to be told or reminded of what happened the night before

Passing out in the middle of a party/gathering/event

In drinking culture, these things are common, frequent, and often considered hilarious. We celebrate and glamorize getting drunk. I'll be bold and say that *none* of these things should be considered normal or funny anymore. They should be huge, bright, flashing red flags. As a parent with children in their tween years, this list is terrifying.

In fact, as a society, we need to radically redefine what "normal drinking" is. (Because how can drinking poison be normal?)

You don't have to be stumbling around with a bottle in a brown paper bag, moments from CPS hauling off your kids, for your drinking to be a problem. You don't have to reach the lowest of lows to claw yourself back out one painful step at a time. You can realize that drinking is not in your best interest and walk away. You can outgrow it any time you're ready.

It doesn't mean you're weak, and it doesn't mean you are "less than." It means you're giving up the effects of a mind-altering, carcinogenic, and addictive drug that is making your life worse instead of better. When you make that decision, you should be celebrated, not shunned!

29

Signs it Might Be Time

I went to the doctor in early 2021 for a physical. When he asked how often I drank, I chuckled and joked about how the pandemic had made us all need to drink a little more often, right? He chuckled back and then moved on when I said I was probably in the three-to-five-drinks-per-week range. In that moment, I believed myself.

I was never honest with myself about how much I was drinking. I would say, "Oh, I have a glass of wine each night with dinner." I bought my own story, which is why it took me so long to open my eyes and notice something wasn't right.

When I forced myself to get brutally honest about how much and how often I was drinking, I realized I was consuming a lot more than I'd been admitting to myself, and certainly enough to be causing plenty of problems.

Consider that the National Institute on Alcohol Abuse and Alcoholism (NIAAA)[1] recommends women limit intake to one drink or less in a day. Heavy drinking (for women) is considered as having four or more drinks in one day or eight or more drinks per week. They go on to explain that heavy drinking markedly increases the likelihood of Alcohol Use Disorder and other alcohol-related harms.

For these guidelines, one drink equals roughly:

> twelve ounces of regular beer
> five ounces of wine
> 1.5 ounces of distilled spirits.

That means a standard bottle of wine has five servings in it. How many of us can say we get five servings out of a bottle? My "one glass with dinner" was more like a ten- to twelve-ounce pour. My "few drinks" at the lake on the weekends were more like four or five a day. The three to five drinks a week I disclosed to my doctor were more like fifteen once I considered the NIAAA guidelines. I was shocked when I paid closer attention and got honest with the numbers.

As you evaluate your drinking, consider what your everyday drinking habits look like. When and how much do you drink throughout the week? Are you drinking a five-ounce glass of wine a few times a week, or are you using an Olivia Pope–sized glass and downing twenty ounces at a time? What do your weekends look like? Do you drink each day, from Friday afternoon through Sunday? What are your patterns?

The morning I woke up with the spins and the hot sweats and ultimately decided I was walking away from alcohol for good, I counted my drinks from the day before and was stunned. No wonder I felt awful. The old head-in-the-sand Hadley would have said, "Oh, I just had a few glasses of wine." The new me realized I'd consumed almost two bottles of rosé.

I can tell you that I now *love* going to the doctor. When they ask how much I drink. I get the biggest kick out of saying, "Oh, I don't, *not at all!*" It's a little thing, but it feels good to know I'm being honest and no longer lying to others *or myself*.

Once you get honest about your drinking habits, it's worth talking about some of the physical signs and symptoms that might be your body's way of waving the white flag and screaming for help. I share these, not as an addiction or recovery expert, but as someone who realized she'd been ignoring them for a long time.

The alcohol we drink is ethanol, and it's toxic. The body recognizes it as a poison and actively rejects it. Alcohol and the byproducts of its metabolism impact almost all the body's systems and organs: the brain, heart, liver, pancreas, skin, immune system, and more. Sometimes, these impacts are pronounced, sometimes they aren't, and we may not know they're happening for a while.

When I drank, I experienced few noticeable physical symptoms other than some righteous hangovers that appeared to be worsening with age. Each year, my hangovers seemed to get angrier and more unbearable. I'd complain about what a bitch it was to get old, like it was an inevitable part of the circle of life.

That hangover I experienced the morning after Eric's '80s surprise party was the first to knock me down so hard that I worried something was wrong with me. My heart was racing, and I was jittery. I was clammy with what I call the "hot chills." I couldn't stop throwing up. I had a headache and felt like my eyeballs were pulsing. My muscles ached so badly I could barely move. My face was puffy, and I looked like I'd been through the zombie apocalypse. I now understand it was my body's way of politely raising its hand and saying, "Hey, I'm going to need you to cut this out."

We make jokes about hangovers and share cures and ways to alleviate the symptoms. Here's the truth: They are a sign you drank too much and your body is not happy. No matter what the ads on your Facebook feed might suggest, there is no way to prevent hangovers except to *not drink ethanol*. Think about how often you're experiencing hangovers and what your symptoms are like. Is it happening once a year, weekly, or almost every day?

If we talk about physical signs that it might be time to cut back, we have to talk about blackouts, and unfortunately, you know this is an area where I have considerable experience. The National Institute for Alcohol Abuse and Alcoholism defines blackouts this way: Alcohol-related blackouts are gaps in a person's memory of events that occurred while they were intoxicated.[2] These gaps happen when a person drinks enough alcohol to temporarily block the transfer of memories from short-term to long-term storage.

When you black out, you're walking around, talking, and behaving as if you're awake, present, and with it. You're not. Blackouts are scary and dangerous, and they significantly increase the risk of bad things happening to you, from sexual assault to cracking your head open in a fall or driving drunk. Not to mention the mystery bruises you're probably waking up with. We joke about blackouts and glorify them, but let's be clear, blacking out is a major sign of trouble.

In the year before I quit, my drinking was more regular than ever, and I was experiencing many negative physical symptoms for the first time. I was *always* tired. I was sleeping horribly and had awful night sweats. I tossed and turned and woke up feeling like I hadn't slept at all. By now, even a single glass of wine would lead to a restless night and a miserable morning.

Alcohol dramatically affects our sleep. We often think of it as a sedative because, initially, it may have a relaxing and drowsy effect. We may fall asleep quickly after drinking (aka pass out), but the quality of our sleep is profoundly and negatively impacted. Binge drinking can be particularly detrimental to sleep quality.

We may sleep, but we're not getting true rest and rejuvenation. And the impact adds up over time.

These were just the signs and symptoms I could *see*. There were undoubtedly other things happening on the inside, too. Other common physical implications of drinking include:

Weight gain

Memory issues/brain fog

Changes in your skin

Getting sick more often

I already mentioned that drinking affects your liver, brain, heart, pancreas, gut, and immune system. Then, I learned that alcohol is now considered a known carcinogen. According to the National Cancer Institute: "The evidence indicates that the more alcohol a person drinks—particularly the more alcohol a person drinks regularly over time—the higher his or her risk is of developing an alcohol-associated cancer. Even those who have no more than one drink per day and binge drinkers (those who consume 4 or more drinks for women and 5 or more drinks for men in one sitting) have a modestly increased risk of some cancers. Based on data from 2009, an estimated 3.5% of cancer deaths in the United States (about 19,500 deaths) were alcohol related."[3]

According to the American Cancer Society[4], drinking alcohol is clearly linked to an increased risk of breast cancer. The risk increases with the amount of alcohol consumed. Women who have 1 alcoholic drink a day have a small (about 7% to 10%) increase in risk compared with those who don't drink, while women who have 2 to 3 drinks a day have about a 20% higher risk. This was a huge eye-opener for me. I couldn't imagine *knowingly* doing something that increases my risk of breast cancer.

With that information in mind, all of these are indications that you might benefit from changing your relationship with alcohol:

Are you experiencing regular hangovers?

Do you black out?

Do you feel constantly exhausted?

How is your sleep quality?

Do you have headaches?

Do you find mystery bruises after drinking?

Have you noticed weight gain or skin issues?

How are your memory and your cognitive skills?

Consider these signs carefully as you weigh your options. Ultimately, you have to decide whether the physical symptoms are worth it. Is drinking that important and so enjoyable that you're willing to sacrifice your physical health and well-being? It's a question only you can answer.

30

Mental Health Red Flags

Besides the physical signs that might indicate that dialing back your drinking would be a good idea, many mental health red flags try to send us messages.

To be clear, I am *not* a mental health professional, and nothing here is a replacement for getting help from one. I'm only relaying some of the commonly known repercussions of drinking. Any tips or suggestions are based on my experience and what has worked for me. I'm a *huge* proponent of raising your hand and asking for help if you need it, so please do that if this topic hits close to home.

I've shared the vicious cycle I experienced the summer I finally pulled the plug on booze. I would spend all week recovering from my weekend hangover, only to repeat the whole thing as soon as I started feeling better. The outward physical symptoms were just another layer on top of what was happening with my mental health during that time.

I noticed an obvious pattern after drinking heavily on the weekend. When I would wake up with a hangover, I would also feel the heavy weight of a depressive episode closing in on me. For several days, I would want to stay in bed and hide. My anxiety was off the charts. I was constantly worrying, stressing, and verging on a spiral into a full-blown panic attack. I felt shaky and on edge. These feelings would peek around Day Three after drinking and then slowly dissipate. I would finally feel better when Friday rolled around, but I would drink again, and the cycle would start over. I had dealt with mild-to-moderate bouts of depression and anxiety for years, but it was always manageable. This feeling was next-level, and it was taking a toll. Sprinkle on the shame, guilt, and regret, and it was a special combination.

As all of this piled on during that last summer, I felt like a shell of a person. I went through the motions but never enjoyed myself, except in that split second after I poured my first glass of wine and convinced myself that all my problems were about to melt away. Fixing your problems with alcohol is like cutting your finger and putting on a Band-Aid dipped in jalapeno juice. Technically, it covers the wound, but it's going to hurt like hell and certainly won't help it heal.

Aside from my personal experience, it's a known fact that alcohol can significantly affect mental health, especially leading to or exacerbating depression and anxiety. The brain is incredibly complex and relies on a delicate balance of chemicals and processes, which alcohol disturbs. Alcohol is a depressant, which means when it disrupts that balance, it affects our thoughts, feelings, emotions, mood, and more. The more we drink, the more impact it seems to have on us. Aside from depression and anxiety, there are more mental health red flags to watch for as you evaluate your relationship with alcohol. I encourage you to take some time to sit with this list of the obvious ones and look inward, thinking about whether any of these things are impacting your mental health and well-being:

Do you have anxiety or depression after drinking or otherwise?

Do you regularly feel shame, guilt, or regret tied to your drinking?

Do you rely on alcohol to do specific "jobs" for you—handling stress, relaxing, socializing?

Does drinking take up a lot of precious mental space in your life?

Do you feel you need alcohol to handle the pressures of life?

How do you typically feel the day after drinking—at peace or uneasy?

This isn't a diagnostic tool. It's only to get you thinking about your own life and whether drinking might be having a negative impact. If you decide it is, it's then up to you to determine what you do with that information.

Once you stop drinking, your mental health issues won't disappear miraculously, although, for me, it almost felt that way. Again, I encourage you to reach out to a professional for help if you're struggling, but cutting back on alcohol may be an essential first step toward the healing and peace you deserve. You deserve to be happy, healthy, and at peace in your own mind. You deserve to not just like yourself but to *love* yourself fully and unconditionally. You deserve to enjoy the life you're living and be free of shame, regret, and fear.

Alcohol had its sneaky tentacles touching almost every part of my mental health. When people comment about how crazy it is that I stopped drinking out of the blue, I argue it had been coming on for years. As I get older, I increasingly value my limited mental and cognitive capital. I'm no longer willing to knowingly limit myself by drinking poison. I sometimes wish I had figured this all out sooner, but I'm celebrating that I am here now, and it keeps getting better.

31

Visualizing a Life with Less Alcohol

For too long, I refused to give up alcohol. Drinking was so embedded in my day-to-day life that it felt impossible to consider untangling it. How would I have fun? How would my introverted self survive in social settings? Would my friends still want to spend time with me? What would that mean for my marriage? And what about the fact that I loved the taste of wine and a margarita on a hot day? Was I just supposed to give all of that up? It felt akin to cutting off a limb, which I can now acknowledge was dramatic and obnoxious.

Most of what I thought I loved about drinking was superficial. None of it made up for the negatives that were piling up. The scale was incredibly unbalanced, but I hung onto the ideas the world feeds us about how important and necessary drinking is.

As I neared my breaking point, I systematically weighed the pros and cons of continuing to drink the way I was.

The pros list went something like this:

> *I love the taste of red wine.*
>
> *I enjoy the ritual of having a glass at the end of the day.*
>
> *It helps me unwind and destress ... for a few minutes.*
>
> *It helps me to be more outgoing and social.*
>
> *It's how I have fun.*

It was a pretty lame list, and it was full of lies.

The cons list was as follows:

> *It's making me depressed and anxious.*
>
> *I constantly feel hungover and unwell.*
>
> *I'm swimming in shame and regret.*
>
> *It's keeping me from being the best parent I can be.*
>
> *I don't like the example I'm setting for my kids.*
>
> *I can't moderate, no matter how hard I try, so I'm always letting myself down.*
>
> *It's ruining my running performance.*
>
> *My skin looks like crap.*
>
> *I'm always tired and rundown.*
>
> *I feel stuck in a vicious cycle.*

Wow. It didn't even feel like a decision when I laid it out like that. The life I could gain by giving up drinking *far* outweighed the meager benefits. I was making myself miserable for no good reason.

I'm not trying to trivialize this decision or imply that it's easy to make these changes. It's not easy, and you have to make the right choice for yourself. Your list might look very different from mine.

I urge you to create your own list of pros and cons. What are the pros of continuing to drink exactly as you are currently? List any you can think of. There are no wrong answers; write the first things that come to mind. Maybe you're a world-renowned wine taster making millions of dollars from your expert palate, or maybe your list of pros looks as silly as mine.

Next, consider the cons of continuing to drink the way you do. List the ways it's hurting your life, your relationships, your health, or your career. That you're here and still reading suggests your con list is probably longer than the pros.

Sometimes, it's eye-opening to see it on paper. Be considerate as you think through your list. You don't need to decide yet—just let it all soak in. Look at your listed pros and cons and consider how they've played out in your life. For me, a pro was that drinking was *so fun*, but in reality, I didn't have a good time. I was miserable more than I enjoyed myself.

Now—close your eyes and visualize the best-case scenario. Picture what your life would look like if you magically eliminated the cons on your list. Think about this in great detail and visualize your day from beginning to end. How would you feel if your life was free of the bad parts of drinking?

Here is what this looked like for me.

I pictured myself waking up at our lake house with a clear head, feeling rested and rejuvenated. I read a book while enjoying my coffee and watching the sunrise over the water. I smiled with gratitude because beauty surrounded me. I was at peace and free of shame and guilt, and I felt good about myself, inside and out. My life was just as I had left it when I went to sleep with a clear head the night before. I felt healthy and content. I enjoyed a long morning run, feeling strong and capable, and coming home to a healthy, nourishing breakfast to start my day. I was present and connected with my boys. I laughed and enjoyed myself as we spent a day on the water. I sat at my computer in the evening, full of ideas and bursting with creativity, ready to write and work on my next book. My day was full of love, joy, peace, and laughter. I went to bed feeling content and at ease in a house with the people I love most.

That was my best-case scenario, and for me, it was simple. It was about liking myself, feeling proud of myself, and being free of shame. It was about enjoying life's simple pleasures with the people I love, without the fog that drinking layered over it all.

Your best-case scenario may look different, and that's fine. The point is to visualize what life with less alcohol would look like in your perfect world. Is that life something you want to work for? Does the life you envisioned feel more fulfilling than the one you're leading currently? You're going to have to make that decision for yourself, but I know you're up for the challenge.

32

Aging Loudly and Gracefully and Forgivingly

I grew up believing aging was a terrifying process to be dreaded. I remember my parents throwing a party for my mom's fortieth birthday, and forty sounded ancient. (Sorry, Mom!) I had a vague notion that our lives, bodies, and minds deteriorate spectacularly with each year past a certain age. Everyone made a big deal about forty, so that was likely the impetus of the downward spiral.

Interestingly, as I approached the dreaded 4-0, I didn't really care. I certainly wasn't kicking and screaming. I used heaps of eye cream and had more gray hair, but I felt at peace with my age and embraced the idea that I could continue improving with each passing year. There was still time to push through the old excuses and misgivings and grow into Hadley 4.0.

I'm getting better at some of the big concepts I used to suck at. I'm finally learning to offer forgiveness, both to myself and others, *and* I refuse to accept bullshit I don't deserve. I'm also learning a mythical superpower that has long evaded me: the ability to say *no* to people and situations that don't serve me. I knew these skills existed as concepts, but I had never mastered them. It was like I had to turn forty to unlock these more advanced levels of this game called life. I'm still no expert, but I'm getting there.

I recently almost said *yes* to a job opportunity that was a horrible fit for me. It didn't mesh with my wants, needs, or skills. It just didn't feel right. But I considered saying yes simply because I felt bad saying no. It would have been a waste of my time and paid me considerably less than I'm worth ... but I didn't want to disappoint a person I'd never met. I finally shook myself and said, "*Hadley*, you know the answer is no. Just tell them and stop even considering this as an option." It felt liberating when I did, even if I still secretly felt guilty for taking up thirty minutes of this person's time to discuss the opportunity. A few years ago, I might have said yes and forced myself to be miserable.

Recognizing that forgiveness, especially self-forgiveness, is more of an art than a science, and is another gift that comes with age. Around the time I turned forty, I realized that life was way too short to hold grudges against myself for the stupid stuff I did in my past. Most of the grievances I'd been holding onto were for things Badley did while she was drinking—memories that make me cringe and want to bang my head on the wall. Since choosing sobriety, a big part of my transformation has been consciously working on forgiving myself for those things. I've learned to stop wasting mental energy on re-hashing mistakes. Learning to gently forgive myself has been difficult but more rewarding than I imagined. I remind myself that my past mistakes do not define me. I'm better because of them. I have to own those mistakes, accept them, forgive them, and then move on, shifting my focus toward doing more things I can feel good about.

Another beautiful perk of aging? I no longer care about trying to fit in. You'll never catch me trying to be something or someone I'm not. I accept and love myself for who I am without apology. I'd rather blaze my own trail and do what's right for *me* than shapeshift to meet others' expectations. I'm not saying it's effortless, but I'm fully committed to being unapologetically ME. Sometimes, I have to remind myself. Sometimes, I have to course-correct. Sometimes, I need to look in the mirror and hype myself up. With age comes the wisdom to catch myself if I stray down a path that's not authentic. Age brings a level of self-awareness that's refreshing and empowering. I can suddenly picture myself as an old lady wearing no pants around the nursing home, simply because they're uncomfortable and I have zero fucks to give.

The timing of all these life changes was perfect and perhaps a product of divine intervention. While I sometimes wish it had happened sooner, my decision to quit drinking was perfectly supported by the age and stage I was at in life. Maybe my efforts at sobriety wouldn't have worked if I was still twenty-nine, trying to fit in with the cool crowd, and afraid to use "no" as a complete sentence. As it often does in retrospect, the timing worked out beautifully, and I don't think I would change a thing.

I am betting I still have at least half my life ahead of me, and I smile to know I'll be sober and clear-headed for it. Being alcohol-free allows me to squeeze the most out of life. It allows me to enjoy all the happy moments and endure the sad. I plan to live the next forty-ish years loudly and joyfully as I get even better at being myself.

33

The Lessons I've Learned

No one knew the inner turmoil I dealt with for years as I floundered through countless attempts to rein things in. All they saw was my picture-perfect mom persona. No one knew I felt constant shame, insecurity, and guilt over my toxic relationship with alcohol. I hid it well.

I'm glad I realized I could change the trajectory of my life by eliminating the one thing causing most of my problems.

I've learned more about myself since choosing to live alcohol-free than I did in my first forty years. The best lesson is that self-love is a lot easier when you actually like yourself. I wake up each day feeling good about who I am as I follow my moral compass. I'm happy and content, and I didn't realize how much booze was robbing me until I quit.

I didn't go to rehab, I didn't have to deal with the physical symptoms of withdrawal, and I haven't gone through any traditional recovery programs. I can't give you a detailed plan for exactly what to do. All I can do is share my story and the tidbits I've learned along the way. I can offer inspiration and promise you that if you're struggling, you're not alone. There are countless ways to reach out and ask for help, and there is no single correct way to recover. That's worth repeating: THERE IS NO PERFECT OR "RIGHT" WAY TO RECOVER. It can be done, though. It might be messy, and it will definitely be imperfect, but it *can* be done. Life can be beautiful and fulfilling without alcohol.

Here are my top ten nuggets of knowledge I learned during what I consider the first year of the rest of my life. I hope they give you hope for what's coming in your life, too, because it's going to be freaking beautiful!

I'm a much more joyful person without alcohol.

The world feels crisper and clearer, like I'm now living in IMAX.

If I need alcohol to have fun doing something, then it's not really fun.

Even on the hard days, I know in my bones I'm doing the right thing.

The people who truly love me will support me.

I would rather feel and experience my emotions than numb them.

I'm not better than anyone who drinks; I'm only better than who I used to be.

I'm capable of so much more than I knew.

I missed a lot when I was drunk, but I'm not missing anything by not drinking.

I'm a better mom, wife, friend, and human without alcohol.

I wish I could go back to the version of Hadley, who woke up on August 6, 2021, suffering from that last hangover, and hug her. I'd tell her to drink some water and push through because big things were about to happen. I never could have guessed my choice would lead to a world of new opportunities. I learned a lot of powerful lessons by just putting one foot in front of the other, one day at a time.

Life won't always be perfect, regardless of your relationship with alcohol, but I know one thing for sure. You *deserve* to be happy. You *deserve* to feel content and proud of yourself. You *deserve* to wake up each day feeling healthy, loved, and fulfilled. You *deserve* to be free of shame and regret and full of forgiveness. If you feel something is off-kilter in your life and alcohol may be part of the problem, listen to your instincts. Please don't ignore them for years as I did. You'll be so damn proud of yourself for stepping into your power and taking back control of your life.

As Glennon Doyle would say, "We can do hard things!" We can; I've seen the proof. I'm living it![1]

Epilogue

I'm writing this on my one-year soberversary. It has been 365 days since I woke up with my last hangover and chose to hit the reset button on my life. It has been a year of courage, vulnerability, struggle, and strength. A year of pouring my heart out on paper as I used my writing to figure out who I was without alcohol. It has been more difficult than I ever imagined, and it has been easier. Mostly, it has been beautiful.

I'll let you in on a secret, though. Much to my dismay, I learned that nothing miraculous happens when you hit the one-year mark. Balloons don't drop from the sky, angels don't sing, and no one presents you with a certificate to congratulate you on completing your journey to an alcohol-free life. There's not even a cake. It's total bullshit.

I guess that's because the work isn't done. Even though it feels momentous, it's just another day. Still, I choose to think of it as a meaningful milestone. It shows how far I've come and how damn proud I am for engineering this change in my life and going after it with my whole heart. I think that deserves to be celebrated and acknowledged.

Some say only a tiny portion of sobriety is about not drinking alcohol. The rest is about doing all the inner work to figure out why you drank in the first place and cleaning up the mess left behind. It's like twenty percent not drinking and eighty percent healing. Things might be a lot easier if those percentages were swapped. For me, the inner work was about accepting myself as an introvert, redefining how to have fun, and finding healthy ways to unwind and cope with stress. For many people, those reasons are much heavier and more difficult to unpack.

I knew in my heart from a young age that something about me and alcohol didn't mesh. I refused to see the bigger picture and listen to my intuition. It was easier to give in to the ease of drinking, so I kept ignoring that inner voice telling me I wasn't supposed to feel so bad. I'll no longer ignore the voice of my intuition telling me when something is off in the balance of my life.

I used to think alcohol was a requirement for any celebration, and now I want to throw a party for each new month I'm alcohol-free. It feels pretty miraculous. We're all capable of whatever changes we want to see in our lives; we just have to go for it. In the meantime, I'll keep celebrating the crap out of every sobriety milestone for as long as I feel like it, and I'll even make my own cake!

Acknowledgements:

I recently helped my parents downsize and came across boxes of my old notebooks from elementary school. There were pages and pages of journal entries, stories, and tall tales that I have absolutely no recollection of creating. I sat on the floor reading them, laughing at their absurdity and embarrassed by most. It was a great reminder that I've loved writing for as long as I have loved reading. Something about putting my thoughts on paper has always helped me process what's happening in my life and my head. It soothes me and helps me make sense of the world. That became especially important as I started this new chapter of life and had to figure out who I was without alcohol after decades as a wine-loving party girl.

Thanks to my amazing mom, I've been devouring books since the moment I could read. Our trips to the library together are some of my earliest and fondest memories. I have always wanted to be an author and to see my own name on a book someday, but it felt like a pie-in-the-sky dream – the type you didn't mention out loud. I had no idea what I might possibly be knowledgeable enough about to write about, but as so often happens, the answer eventually made itself clear.

It speaks to the quality of the people in my life that absolutely no one so much as flinched when I said I was writing this book. My husband, Eric, my mom, and my ride-or-die friends have cheered me on from the beginning. My best friend's first response was, "Let's plan our outfits for The Today Show!"

They knew I could do it even before I did. They've been my early readers, my sounding boards, and my therapists. They not only supported my choice to quit drinking but also my choice to share the story with the world. They went through every step of this process with me, and they reminded me to believe in myself in the moments when belief was in short supply.

A huge thank you to all of you – you know who you are.

None of this would have happened without my husband's unwavering support. His unconditional love is legendary. Eric – you're one of the good ones and I consider myself blessed. Thank you for having faith in me and my dreams.

I'm also incredibly grateful for the honesty and openness this process has brought to my relationship with my boys. Writing this book has encouraged me to have tough conversations with them and to teach them the power of vulnerability, forgiving ourselves, and overcoming our mistakes. It has brought us closer, and the support they've shown blows my mind.

For now, at least, they're not embarrassed that I'm out there on social media, boldly talking about my experience and the lessons I've learned through sobriety. They've proposed titles and cover ideas, they've helped film for my social media content, and they've told all of their teachers about my book. They're proud of me, and that might be the best feeling in the world.

I would also like to thank Donna Mosher and Lisa Hagan, who believed in this project even when it still needed a *lot* of work. They "got" me from the beginning and helped guide me through the publishing world with infinite patience. Their expertise and perspectives were invaluable. Thank you for helping me tell my story in a way that works and for allowing me to share it with the world.

Finally, to all of the women out there who are struggling in silence, please use my words as your permission slip to own your story and your truth. If something about your drinking doesn't feel right, don't ignore that feeling. You deserve a life that is full and beautiful. If alcohol is keeping you from that life, don't waste another minute making excuses for it!

Endnotes

Chapter 9

1. Jolene Park, "Gray Area Drinking," November 2017 in Denver, Colorado, TED video, https://www.ted.com/talks/jolene_park_gray_area_drinking?language=en

2. Annie Grace, *This Naked Mind: Control Alcohol, Find Freedom, Discover Happiness & Change Your Life* (Avery, 2015), Chapter 13, The Mystery of Spontaneous Sobriety.

Chapter 12

1. Centers for Disease Control and Prevention, *Dietary Guidelines for Alcohol*, Revised April 2022, https://www.cdc.gov/alcohol/fact-sheets/moderate-drinking.htm#:~:text=To%20reduce%20the%20risk%20of,days%20when%20alcohol%20is%20consumed.

Chapter 15

1. Brené Brown, *Dare to Lead: Brave Work. Tough Conversations. Whole Hearts.* (Random House, 2018), page 126.

Chapter 16

1. Brené Brown, *Atlas of the Heart: Mapping Meaningful Connection and the Language of Human Experience* (Random House, 2021), page 52.

Chapter 17

1. National Institute on Alcohol and Alcoholism, *Early Drinking Linked to Higher Lifetime Alcoholism Risk, 2006*, https://www.niaaa.nih.gov/news-events/news-releases/early-drinking-linked-higher-lifetime-alcoholism-risk and National Institute on Alcohol and Alcoholism, *Get the Facts About Underage Drinking*, https://www.niaaa.nih.gov/publications/brochures-and-fact-sheets/underage-drinking

Chapter 24

1. Harvard Health Publishing, *How does exercise reduce stress? Surprising answers to this question and more*, 2020, https://www.health.harvard.edu/staying-healthy/exercising-to-relax#:~:text=The%20mental%20benefits%20of%20aerobic,natural%20painkillers%20and%20mood%20elevators.

Chapter 29

1. National Institute on Alcohol and Alcoholism, *The Basics: Defining How Much Alcohol is Too Much*, Revised 2024, https://www.niaaa.nih.gov/health-professionals-communities/core-resource-on-alcohol/basics-defining-how-much-alcohol-too-much#pub-toc3

2. National Institute on Alcohol and Alcoholism, *Interrupted Memories: Alcohol-Induced Blackouts*, Revised 2023, https://www.niaaa.nih.gov/publications/brochures-and-fact-sheets/interrupted-memories-alcohol-induced-blackouts

3. National Cancer Institute, Alcohol and Cancer Risk, Updated 2021, https://www.cancer.gov/about-cancer/causes-prevention/risk/alcohol/alcohol-fact-sheet#what-is-the-evidence-that-alcohol-drinking-can-cause-cancer

4. American Cancer Society, *Lifestyle-related Breast Cancer Risk Factors*, Updated 2022, https://www.cancer.org/cancer/types/breast-cancer/risk-and-prevention/lifestyle-related-breast-cancer-risk-factors.html

Chapter 33

1. Glennon Doyle, *Untamed* (The Dial Press, 2020), page 85

Author Biography

Hadley resides in the Washington, DC, area with her husband and a house full of boys. She's fluent in potty humor and depends on her dog, Maya, as the only other female in the house.

An avid runner and reader and a one-woman sobriety hype squad on social media, working hard to spread the message that anyone can quit drinking at any time, for any reason.

As a lifelong fitness enthusiast and coach for many years, she was very good at preaching about the essentials of a healthy lifestyle. She even built a whole brand around her love of wine and fitness. The dirty truth was that she was neglecting her own health. Alcohol was a dark cloud that followed her for most of her life, always lurking in the shadows. Ever since her first sip at fourteen, something about her relationship with booze felt corrupt in a way she couldn't articulate. It turned out that no amount of exercise or eating kale and quinoa could negate the damage drinking was doing to her body and mind.

On the outside, she was killing it, and that's what the world saw. People assumed she had her act together, and she did nothing to dissuade them. On the inside, she was barely hanging on by a thread.

Her problem with drinking wasn't extreme; she wasn't physically dependent, and she wasn't even close to the stereotypical rock bottom. She drank the same way everyone around her did: graduating from the college binge-drinking scene straight to the mommy wine scene. It was the typical suburban woman's trajectory. "Normal" social drinker or not, alcohol had a stranglehold on her that she didn't like. She was riddled with shame and self-loathing. She felt like she was the only person experiencing these tumultuous feelings tied to booze, which made her feel broken and alone.

In 2021, she reached her breaking point after a series of escalating drinking episodes and the resulting deterioration of her mental health. One morning, after too much rosé, she woke up with hot chills and a pounding headache. She knew it was time, and she made the scary decision to stop drinking. Her heart screamed that it was the right choice. Instead of feeling like she was making a sacrifice, it felt like a new door was opening.

Hadley spent the next year figuring out who she was without alcohol and learning to navigate a world that seemed to revolve around it. She began to document her experience, and before she fully realized what was happening, this book was born. She continues to share her story with the hope that it reaches other women who are stuck in that drinking gray area where she floundered for so many years.

Printed in Great Britain
by Amazon

57280205R00106